pra

LIVING A LIFE THAT MATTERS: 7 KEYS FOR PURPOSEFUL LIVING

"Val Hale's new book, *Living a Life That Matters: 7 Keys for Purposeful Living*, is a must-read. Each principle is profound and impactful, and I look forward to applying these principles to business as well. I will return to this book many times."

—*Cheryl D. Snapp Conner, founder and CEO of SnappConner PR*

"Here's what I learned from *Living a Life That Matters*: You don't need money to be happy, to forgive, to be gracious, to be kind, and to build amazing relationships with those you love. Val's 7 keys will unlock the windows of heaven."

—*Vai Sikahema, NBC Philadelphia news anchor and two-time NFL pro bowler*

"It's about time that one of my favorite and most exemplary people shared his personal formula for a successful life. Val's unsurpassed class, dignity, and selflessness—especially in the face of setbacks—makes his wisdom in these pages all the more invaluable. A 'quiet professional' with the stealth of a Navy Seal, Val is often observing in the background, trusted by everyone, and ensuring the success of others' missions. That's why he's a sought-after leader. His timely and personal message is profoundly universal, yet simple. This is a must-read book for anyone seeking to make the most out of every minute, personally and professionally!"

—*Sharlene Wells Hawkes, businesswoman, former Miss America and ESPN reporter*

"Val has been a great friend for decades and has always demonstrated his desire to live a life that matters. As a family man and a professional, he appropriately shares his light throughout this book by revealing stories and anecdotes that will improve your life."

—*Chad Lewis, athletic administrator, former NFL all-pro tight end and three-time pro bowler*

living a life
THAT MATTERS

7
KEYS
for
PURPOSEFUL
LIVING

VAL HALE

Plain Sight Publishing, an Imprint of Cedar Fort, Inc. • Springville, Utah

To Nancy, Chris, Brandon, Rachel, and their spouses and children, whose lives and happiness matter most to me.

The opinions and views expressed herein belong solely to the author and do not necessarily represent the opinions or views of Cedar Fort, Inc. Permission for the use of sources, graphics, and photos is also solely the responsibility of the author.

ISBN 13: 978-1-4621-1704-8

Published by Plain Sight Publishing, an imprint of Cedar Fort, Inc.,
2373 W. 700 S., Springville, UT 84663
Distributed by Cedar Fort, Inc., www.cedarfort.com

LIBRARY OF CONGRESS CATALOGING-IN-PUBLICATION DATA
Hale, Val, 1957- author.
 Living a life that matters : 7 keys for purposeful living / Val Hale.
    pages cm
 Includes bibliographical references.
 ISBN 978-1-4621-1704-8 (perfect bound : alk. paper)
  1. Christian life--Mormon authors. 2. Life--Religious aspects--Christianity. 3. Meaning (Philosophy)--Religious aspects. I. Title.
 BX8656.H347 2015
 248.4'89332--dc23
                                  2015027443

Cover design by Lauren Error
Cover design © 2015 by Lyle Mortimer
Edited and typeset by Eileen Leavitt

Printed in the United States of America

10 9 8 7 6 5 4 3 2 1

Printed on acid-free paper

contents

introduction

Every life matters.

Every person has a contribution to make.

God has given each of us unique talents and abilities. How we choose to use them will determine how impactful our lives will be within our sphere of influence.

We all desire to live happy, fulfilling, purposeful lives. The Founding Fathers acknowledged that the "pursuit of happiness" is a God-given right and a fundamental reason for our existence.

Each of us goes about pursuing and finding joy and fulfillment in different ways. We come from varying circumstances and backgrounds. Our upbringing and culture help shape our view of life and oftentimes determine our financial and socioeconomic circumstances. I think most of us, at one time or another, have believed, like Tevya in *Fiddler on the Roof,* that our problems would somehow be solved "if [we] were very, very rich."[1]

While having money can oftentimes make life easier, it is by no means the solution to joy and fulfillment. Living a purposeful, fulfilling life can be achieved with little or no money. I learned this lesson from a great man named Charlie Bates many years ago when I was first married.

Charlie was the ecclesiastical leader assigned to oversee a flock of newlywed students. He was a good man who had built a successful and prosperous business. He had been named Utah's Businessman of the Year a few years prior to my getting to know him, and he certainly enjoyed the trappings of success. He had a big, beautiful home with hardwood floors and nice rugs throughout. He had a well-manicured yard with a swimming pool. I suspect there was little materially for which he wanted.

I was a poor college student living with my new bride in a basement apartment. Somehow, I ended up with the assignment to visit Charlie each month. I would go to his home with another student to visit him and his wife and leave an inspirational message. I must confess it was intimidating for me to visit this important, successful man in his home, but he always welcomed us warmly with open arms.

On one of our visits, I was sitting on his nice couch admiring the furniture and decorations in his living room. I awkwardly blurted out how nice it must be to have such a beautiful house full of so many impressive things.

Charlie laughed and then taught me a great lesson.

"Val," he said, "as I look back on my life, the time my wife and I were happiest was when we were your age doing what you are doing. We were newly married, going to school, and poor as church mice. We lived in a basement apartment and wondered how we would manage to pay the bills. But we had each other, and we were madly in love and had our whole lives in front of us. Despite the difficult circumstances, we were happier then than we have ever been."

He continued, "I can honestly tell you that the more money I have made, the more problems I have had to deal with. So, don't envy my lifestyle. Enjoy this time in your life, because you really have everything you need to be happy."

It is true that we have everything we need to be happy in life and make a difference in the world. Both happiness and purposefulness are attitudes. We can choose them or their alternative. A favorite quote of mine by Judith Knowlton says, "I discovered I always have choices, and sometimes it's only a choice of attitude."[2]

Besides developing an attitude of happiness and intentional living, I believe there are certain keys, ingredients, or principles—whatever you choose to call them—that lead to a fulfilling and purposeful life. In these pages, I hope to share what I have discovered those keys to be. I draw heavily from personal experiences. I don't have a PhD in sociology or psychology, so you may be disappointed if you are expecting a book filled with scientific research. I have lived a rich life and have followed contemporary philosopher Yogi Berra's advice: "You can observe a lot by watching."[3]

In 1979, I attended a meeting at which a well-known religious and civic leader was speaking. It was an influential time in my life. I was in college trying to determine what I wanted to do for a career. I was becoming serious about getting married and was excited—yet anxious—about the future.

This leader gave some great counsel to those young people in attendance. During his talk, he read a quote that stood out to me and has had a powerful impact throughout my life. I have repeated it many times in talks and lessons. In fact, the saying influenced this book.

"Happy is the man who has found his *worship*, his *wife*, and his *work* and loves all three."[4]

The longer I live and the more I experience life, the more I realize that the above statement is true. Those are three key ingredients for a happy, fulfilling life. But I also realize there are additional keys if we want to live life to its fullest and experience the maximum joy and opportunities for growth and influence it can offer.

I want to acknowledge up front that someone who is lacking one or two of the keys mentioned in this book will not be precluded from enjoying life and accomplishing significant things. I firmly believe people tend to make the best of what they have. There are countless stories of people who never married who are happy and successful. There are people who had jobs they didn't particularly enjoy but found ways to live a full life anyway. And there are plenty of nonreligious folks who enjoy life and make a positive difference in the world.

My point in writing this book is to highlight those principles and concepts I believe enrich and bless our lives, add to its fulfillment, and help us become the best we can be. Can you be happy and successful without one or two of them? Sure. But I believe the life that includes all seven of these keys will be richer, more meaningful, and more purposeful than the life that doesn't. They are, I believe, ageless principles that are true regardless of contemporary beliefs or societal shifts in philosophy.

Living a purposeful life is not easy. In fact, the difference between a life that is purposeful and one that isn't usually boils down to intention and determination. A purposeful life is intentional. It is focused and goal driven. It requires effort and direction. A non-purposeful life just happens. It takes things as they come along with no forethought or planning.

Hopefully, after reading this book, you will be inspired to improve in the seven identified areas and will experience more joy as a result. I hope you will look at your life and determine what you can do to make it more meaningful and impactful.

It will be worth the effort.

NOTES

1. "If I Were a Rich Man," *Fiddler on the Roof*, musical by Jerry Bock, lyrics by Sheldon Harnick, 1964.

2. Judith Knowlton, accessed September 29, 2015, https://www.mindbloom.com/apps/inspiration/detail/quote/2bb2be22-6d99-4764-a7ae-dbdf29485d07/.

3. Yogi Berra and Dave Kaplan, *You Can Observe a Lot by Watching: What I've Learned About Teamwork From the Yankees and Life* (Hoboken, NJ: John Wiley & Sons, 2008).

4. "In His Steps," Ezra Taft Benson, speech given at Brigham Young University, March 4, 1979.

be a doer, not a spectator

**LET US, THEN, BE UP AND DOING,
WITH A HEART FOR ANY FATE;
STILL ACHIEVING, STILL PURSUING,
LEARN TO LABOR AND TO WAIT.[1]**

—HENRY WADSWORTH LONGFELLOW

When I was a sophomore in high school, I played on the school's football team. My coach was a man named Al Davis. Despite being what I would classify as a peculiar person, he was a great coach. Years before, he had coached college football but had somehow managed to end up coaching the sophomores at my high school, much to our good fortune.

I usually tried to avoid personal interaction with Coach Davis. He was serious and gruff enough that I tried to keep my distance. One afternoon, however, I ran into him walking behind the bleachers. He stopped to talk to me. I doubt he knew my name because he always called me "Tiger."

Lacking anything constructive to say and feeling somewhat intimidated, I asked if he would be going to the college football game on Saturday. I was a huge sports fan and attended every sporting event I possibly could. And since Coach Davis was a coach and had coached college football, I assumed he would be there. His answer surprised me and taught me a great lesson.

"No," he said. "I don't go to events as a spectator. I much prefer to enjoy an activity I can participate in rather than go watch others play a game or do something."

At the time, I shook my head in disbelief as he walked away. I could not understand how someone—especially a coach—could swear off sporting events. Didn't everyone eat, drink, and breathe sports like I did?

Two years later, I transferred into a recreation class taught by Coach

Davis. I didn't know much about it, other than it sounded fun and many of my friends talked about it. That turned out to be the most useful and life-changing class of my high school experience. Over the course of the next few months, we learned how to do freestyle skiing, cross-country skiing, photography, bowling, golf, fly-fishing, and fly tying, among other things. I loved going to that class.

I watched Al Davis in action as a teacher. I could tell he loved doing the activities he taught us. After work or on weekends, he would head up the nearby Provo River to catch and release five-pound brown trout on flies he had tied himself. He was a fantastic skier and golfer. He loved to hike in and photograph the nearby mountains. In fact, when he unexpectedly died during surgery a number of years later, his students installed a plaque for him in a beautiful cirque above Sundance Resort on the backside of Mount Timpanogos, a mountain where he frequently took them to meditate and write in their journals. The plaque was inscribed with these words, uttered on many occasions by Coach Davis to his students:

**Self-fulfillment begins
when self-pity ends.
Go for it.**

Although I was too poor to purchase equipment for or participate in most of the activities we learned in Mr. Davis' recreation class, I developed a love for them. Years later, when I had more time and money, I took up every one of those activities and still pursue them to this day. They have become my hobbies and passion away from work. I escape to them to relieve my stress. I will be forever grateful to Al Davis for introducing me not only to those fun activities but, more important, to the notion that it is better to do than to watch.

WE HAVE BECOME A SOCIETY OF SPECTATORS

Today we live in a spectator society. So much of what we do involves watching others do things. We watch sporting events on TV or in person. We watch other people make fools of themselves on reality TV. We spend time observing what our friends are up to on Facebook and Twitter. The Nielsen Corporation—the experts who measure and report our TV-watching habits—found that, on average, Americans watch approximately 153 hours of television at home per month, or about five hours per day.[2] That means the average American spends approximately one week of every month in front of the television screen.

Let's say the average American spends eight hours a day sleeping and eight hours a day at work or school. That leaves about eight hours of discretionary time. Nielsen is telling us most Americans spend nearly three-fourths of that "free" time in front of a television.

That statistic is troubling in so many ways. Those hours sitting idly watching TV are essentially "lost." Some people will argue TV can be educational and that they like to relax and unwind after work. I can understand some of that. I, too, like to watch an occasional show or sporting event or the news. But spending four to five hours a night watching TV is excessive. Imagine what a person could accomplish with thirty-five hours a week. How many books could be read or written? What fun or useful skills could be learned? Think of the quality parenting that could be done if Mom and Dad turned off the TV and actually did something with the kids.

The simple truth is that if we want to live a life that is truly purposeful, fulfilling, and impactful, we must fill it with action and activity. The act of passive spectating that is sweeping the world has nothing redeeming about it. Taking the time that God has given us each day and using it for acts of kindness and service, worthwhile and uplifting pursuits, and opportunities to interact with those we love is a profitable exchange.

Even the Bible advances the idea that it is better to be active participants rather than passive spectators when it counsels us, "Be ye doers of the word, and not hearers only" (James 1:22).

Years ago, I read a story in *Reader's Digest* magazine that teaches the impact of spending time doing things with our families. The story has always been one of my favorites. Granted, it took place in an era before TV, but the message is still the same: we need to make the effort to do things and create memories with our loved ones.

Francis Fowler tells of a day when her mother and father, along with some other adults in the neighborhood, spontaneously set aside their Saturday chores to join their children flying kites. They spent most of the day sending the kites soaring heavenward and reeling them in again and again.

It was one of those magical, unforgettable days, but no one spoke of it again for many years. Francis often thought of it and how those moments outside had brought her closer to her parents. She even compared that moment to the kingdom of heaven, and at times she felt guilty about how strong her feelings and memories were about it.

The irony was that several times throughout her later life when she was conversing with people who had been there on that day, they all brought up how impactful that moment in time had been for them. All involved had experienced a slice of heaven in the spontaneity of frolicking around the park with kites.[3]

SPONTANEITY CREATES FUN, LASTING MEMORIES

How many times do we as parents state that we are too busy to get out and actually do something with our children? Creating memories for them and us really requires just a little effort. Looking back, the memories that stand out most vividly about my interaction with my children are the times I decided to do something on the spur of the moment. Some of my most impactful times as a parent were when I decided to get outside my comfort zone and do something out of the ordinary with my family.

On one such occasion, I was sitting in the barbershop waiting to get my hair cut. Like most barbershops, there were dozens of old magazines lying around. I happened to pick up an *Arizona Highways* magazine and started thumbing through it. I was raised in Arizona, so that magazine has always had tremendous appeal to me.

As I flipped through the pages, I came across a story and photos of the waterfalls located in the Havasupai Indian reservation. These waterfalls at the bottom of the Grand Canyon are breathtakingly beautiful. Several of my friends had made the ten-mile hike down the south rim of the Grand Canyon to experience the falls and had spoken glowingly about their pristine beauty. Sitting there, I had a sudden desire to take my family on a journey to Havasupai.

That urge to go hiking and camping came only a couple of days before the Memorial Day weekend. I got some contact information about Havasupai from the magazine and started making calls. I knew they limited the number of people who were allowed to hike to the falls. And I knew reservations were at times hard to come by. Memorial Day weekend, I thought, would be an especially busy time because it was the prime time before the summer heat made the trip almost unbearable. Nevertheless, I placed the call.

I was told we would be able to get reservations if we hiked into the falls on Memorial Day. Most people, they explained, would be leaving on Memorial Day. So I went to my wife and children with the proposal of a whirlwind trip to Havasupai.

They loved the idea. Fortunately, I have a wife who, although not as spontaneous as I, loves to backpack and camp. And my children also love adventure, so convincing them and getting them excited for the journey was fairly easy. My oldest son, about fourteen at the time, even recruited one of his friends to come along. We drove to Las Vegas, where we stayed in a hotel. Then we drove the remaining few hours to the parking lot at the top of the canyon's rim, where we slept in our sleeping bags beside our vehicle.

At 4:00 a.m. on Memorial Day, we awoke and began the descent into the Grand Canyon. There are no roads into Havasupai. The only way to get there is to hike, ride a horse or mule, or fly in a helicopter. It is the only town in America where they actually deliver the mail by mule.

We hiked the ten miles to the falls and set up camp. For the rest of that day and half the next, we explored some of God's most beautiful creations on this earth and created lifelong memories with our children. To this day, they still talk about it. They laugh about how Dad got sick climbing out of the canyon and they had to "rescue" him. They talk about how strenuous the climb was. But mostly they just reminisce about what a fantastic time we had as a family enjoying each other and nature.

Our backpacking trip to Havasu Falls in the Grand Canyon introduced our children to backpacking and showed them that they could do hard things.

Those memories will be in our family forever because I acted on a sudden impulse to go on an adventure I had always wanted to attempt. It didn't require a lot of planning. It didn't require a significant amount of money. It was just a matter of deciding to do it and then following through.

A few years later, in 1998, we had a similar experience, except this time it was over the Fourth of July. A day or so before the Fourth, we found out our children, who were teenagers at the time, didn't have any commitments for that day. That was rare, indeed. So my wife and I decided we should take the family on another adventure. We had no idea what we would do. We just wanted to go somewhere with the kids. For some reason, I thought it would be fun to visit Jackson Hole, Wyoming.

I called the hotels. All the rooms were booked. I called the campgrounds. They were all full—with one exception. The KOA campground told me the only thing they had available was a teepee.

"A what?" I asked, stifling a laugh.

"It's a real teepee, just like the Indians lived in," responded the person on the telephone. "It can sleep about six to eight people."

"We'll take it," I stated as I smiled, envisioning my teenage children sleeping in a teepee. After all, what parent doesn't secretly enjoy keeping his or her teenagers humble?

We had an incredible time in Jackson Hole. We went rafting down the Snake River. We watched a spectacular fireworks show. We ate delicious food. But the thing my wife and children still laugh about to this day is sleeping in that teepee. They love to tell their friends about the time their crazy dad took the family to Jackson Hole and made them sleep

The infamous Jackson Hole teepee will always be a symbol of Dad's craziness and a cause for laughter in our family.

in a teepee. In fact, every time someone in our family mentions Jackson Hole, the teepee story is revived. A short while ago, my son had to go through Jackson Hole for work. Before he went, he recounted to his children and wife the infamous trip and teepee lodging. Quite honestly, I would not be surprised if that story is repeated at my funeral.

BEING A PARTICIPANT REQUIRES EFFORT

One of the reasons we tend to be spectators is because it is much easier than being a participant. Spectating requires very little investment other than time. When you are a spectator, you don't have to plan and exert the energy needed to carry out an activity. You also don't have to take the risks associated with being a participant. Getting out and doing carries with it some risk. Skiing down a mountain or riding a mountain bike along a steep trail are inherently dangerous. Sitting on a couch isn't. It goes back to the well-known saying, "A ship in harbor is safe, but that is not what ships are made for." [4]

Likewise, human beings are safe on couches, but that's not what humans are for.

The beauty about *doing* is that it can be done without a lot of money. The most important "doing" ingredient is creativity. Anyone, poor or rich, can think of interesting things to do. Granted, in some communities it may be easier to find accessible activities than in others. But even if you live in the most remote place on earth, there are still plenty of things to do. Especially with the Internet, it is easy to find things to do and things to make. There are plenty of fun things to learn and do right at your fingertips.

I am a believer that a "doing" mentality can be cultivated by parents who engage their children in activities at an early age. Going to the library or the museum on a regular basis creates anticipation in kids. They look forward to going on their excursion. They talk about it and plan for it. Sometimes the anticipation of doing something is almost more enjoyable than actually carrying it out. I realize that is somewhat contradictory to my previous statement about the merits of spontaneity, but both planned activities and spontaneous ones have value.

A father who tells his son he plans to take him to a big upcoming football game will create in that boy a sense of excitement that will build each passing day. When the big day finally arrives, it will be like Christmas morning for the child. The game may end up being somewhat disappointing because of bad weather or the wrong team winning or poor seat location, but those things notwithstanding, the excursion will have been a success because of the thrill of anticipation.

How often have you gone on a long-awaited, much-anticipated trip and upon your arrival at home declared, "I really need a vacation"? The best part of the entire experience often is the planning and contemplating. The "doing" is fun too, but it requires a significant expenditure of energy.

DOING THINGS WITH FAMILY IS
BETTER THAN HAVING THINGS

Our family moved to Salt Lake City when I was twelve years old. In my neighborhood lived a family that was always doing things together. They were fairly well to do and had lots of "toys" like boats, campers, and so on. I learned their father had done well in his profession and had come into a lot of money. He considered building a nicer, bigger home, but the family sat down together and talked about the pros and cons of doing so. The father explained that one option would be to stay in the current, smaller home and use the money they would have spent on a bigger home to purchase toys the family could use to spend time together.

After weighing the options, that is what they decided to do. The main thing I remember about that family is that they were always having fun together, going places and participating in activities. Sure, they had plenty of toys, but they made the effort to go do something. There are many people who have lots of toys but don't take the time to use them with their family and loved ones. I also know many people who don't have resources to buy toys, but they find ways to create memories and experiences in their lives. They find ways to do memorable activities with their friends and families.

While growing up in a small town in northeastern Arizona, my family couldn't afford TV. Our town was far enough away from Phoenix that the only way we could get TV was through cable. And cable TV cost money, which we didn't have. Consequently, watching TV was not an option for me, unless it was at a friend's house. That forced me to go out and find things to do.

Looking back, I can't imagine a better blessing than being raised without TV. Unlike many kids, I really didn't have a chance to be a couch potato. I also had seven sisters and, for much of my childhood, no brothers. So I was constantly on the lookout for fun things to do in the neighborhood and throughout town. My best friends, Evan and Ivan, would frequently join me in search of adventures. We had a childhood that, in many ways, would make Mark Twain jealous. I don't even dare tell some of the stories of things we did for fear my grandkids would try to duplicate them.

I suppose we had our moments of idleness. We played a lot of mumbly peg, a game in which you try to repeatedly stick a knife in the ground by tossing it off your fingers, arms, shoulders, or head. We spent a lot of time sitting up high on tree limbs watching clouds parade by. But most of our days were spent doing chores or riding horses or riding our bikes around town or shooting our BB guns or building tree houses or underground forts. When I look back on my youth, I marvel at all the things my friends and I did before the age of twelve. We loved life and wanted to participate in as many adventures as we could.

The fact that I grew up *doing* set the course for the rest of my life.

Henry Wadsworth Longfellow talks about the importance of being a doer in his classic poem "A Psalm of Life."

A Psalm of Life
By Henry Wadsworth Longfellow

Tell me not, in mournful numbers,
Life is but an empty dream! —
For the soul is dead that slumbers,
And things are not what they seem.
Life is real! Life is earnest!
And the grave is not its goal;
Dust thou art, to dust returnest,
Was not spoken of the soul.
Not enjoyment, and not sorrow,
Is our destined end or way;
But to act, that each to-morrow
Find us farther than to-day.
Art is long, and Time is fleeting,
And our hearts, though stout and brave,
Still, like muffled drums, are beating
Funeral marches to the grave.
In the world's broad field of battle,
In the bivouac of Life,
Be not like dumb, driven cattle!
Be a hero in the strife!
Trust no Future, howe'er pleasant!
Let the dead Past bury its dead!
Act, — act in the living Present!
Heart within, and God o'erhead!
Lives of great men all remind us
We can make our lives sublime,
And, departing, leave behind us
Footprints on the sands of time;

Footprints, that perhaps another,
Sailing o'er life's solemn main
A forlorn and shipwrecked brother,
Seeing, shall take heart again.
Let us, then, be up and doing,
With a heart for any fate;
Still achieving, still pursuing,
Learn to labor and to wait.[5]

Years ago I heard a brief essay entitled "The Station" by Robert Hastings. I was so impressed by the essay that I copied it and put it inside my day planner, where I could see it every day and be reminded of its valuable message of cherishing each moment of each day and not awaiting some future event to be happy in life.

The Station
By Robert Hastings (used here with permission)

Tucked away in our subconscious minds is an idyllic vision. We see ourselves on a long, long trip that almost spans the continent. We're traveling by passenger train, and out the windows we drink in the passing scene of cars on nearby highways, of children waving at a crossing, of cattle grazing on a distant hillside, of smoke pouring from a power plant, of row upon row of corn and wheat, of flatlands and valleys, of mountains and rolling hillsides, of city skylines and village halls, of biting winter and blazing summer and cavorting spring and docile fall.

But uppermost in our minds is the final destination. On a certain day at a certain hour we will pull into the station. There will be bands playing and flags waving. And once we get there so many wonderful dreams will come true. So many wishes will be fulfilled and so many pieces of our lives finally will be neatly fitted together like a completed jigsaw puzzle. How restlessly we pace the aisles, damming the minutes for loitering, waiting, waiting, waiting for the station.

However, sooner or later we must realize there is no one station, no one place to arrive at once and for all. The true joy of life is the trip. The station is only a dream. It constantly outdistances us.

When we get to the station that will be it!" we cry. Translated it means, "When I'm 18 that will be it! When I buy a new 450 SL Mercedes Benz, that will be it! When I put the last kid through college that will be it! When I have paid off the mortgage that will be it! When I win a promotion that will be it! When I reach the age of retirement that will be it! I shall live happily ever after!"

Unfortunately, once we get "it," then "it" disappears. The station somehow hides itself at the end of an endless track.

"Relish the moment" is a good motto, especially when coupled with Psalm 118:24: "This is the day which the Lord hath made; we will rejoice and be glad in it." It isn't the burdens of today that drive men mad. Rather, it is regret over yesterday or fear of tomorrow. Regret and fear are twin thieves who would rob us of today.

So, stop pacing the aisles and counting the miles. Instead, climb more mountains, eat more ice cream, go barefoot more often, swim more rivers, watch more sunsets, laugh more, and cry less. Life must be lived as we go along. The station will come soon enough.[6]

USE GOD'S GIFT OF TIME TO ACCOMPLISH SOMETHING

Truly, life is to be savored and enjoyed. The one thing we have all been given—the only thing we all have in common—is the gift of time. Every person on this earth has twenty-four hours to use in a day. The thing that distinguishes us from each other is what we choose to do with that time. In fact, the quality of our life will depend, in large part, on how we utilize each of those minutes.

I have always maintained that early morning is when our minds are clearest and most focused. The challenge is exercising "mind over mattress" so we can climb out of bed and get the day started in a productive manner. It is so easy to roll over and hit the snooze button because we are tired. Sleep is a desirable commodity for most of us. I used to set my alarm clock across the room from my bed so I would have to actually get out of bed to turn it off. Currently, my clock is on my bedside table, so I too often succumb to the snooze button.

There are other decisions we make that have a big impact on how much time we have during the day to accomplish things. One of the most significant time drains is driving to and from work. Choosing where we live can save or expend a significant amount of time in our lives. A friend of mine once told me he commuted two hours each way to work in New York City. That's four hours a day just getting to and from his place of employment. What a sacrifice!

The current Lt. Governor of Utah, Spencer Cox, lives in Fairview, Utah, and commutes two hundred miles round-trip each day to the Capitol in Salt Lake City. He wants his children to have the advantage of growing up on a farm and in a small community. He feels so strongly about it that he commutes nearly four hours each day. He knows that his current responsibility is temporary, so he is willing to sacrifice his time so his family can enjoy a country lifestyle.

I learned a valuable lesson about commuting in 1978 from G. Homer Durham, a very bright man who had served as president of Arizona State University and commissioner of higher education in Utah. He had come to Chile, where I was finishing my two-year service as a missionary for The Church of Jesus Christ of Latter-day Saints, to speak to the missionaries and members of the Church. I was assigned to be his chauffer and translator, so I spent some time alone with him in the car, where I had a chance to ask him questions.

One day, as we were driving along, I turned to him and asked, "Elder Durham, I will be going back to the United State in a couple of weeks to continue my life there. What advice do you have to help me be as successful as I can be?"

Now keep in mind that this was one of the smartest men I had ever met. He was brilliant. He had been an educational leader and a spiritual leader throughout his life. He was about as close as I could find to a guru at the top of a mountain. I just knew he would give me a profound answer—some deep philosophical guidance that would lead me to a lifetime of happiness and success, and I anxiously awaited his answer.

He didn't respond immediately. He thought for a minute, and then his answer caught me completely off guard.

"I would suggest," he began slowly, "that you live close to where you work so you don't spend all your spare time commuting."

That was it?! That was his answer? It was the last thing I expected him to say. There was no spiritual guidance or encouragement to major in this or that in college. There was no deep philosophical treatise. Instead, he told me to live close to where I work!

I must confess I was more than a little surprised and disappointed by his answer at the time. But as I have grown older, I see the wisdom in what he was telling me. He was teaching me to make the most of every minute of time God has given me. I followed his advice and, for most of my working career, I have lived within ten minutes of the office. That has given me more time to be with my family and has allowed me to participate in more activities and do more community service. It is something simple, yet life changing, to not have to spend a lot of time driving to and from work.

I recently accepted an offer from Utah's current governor, Gary

Herbert, to work in his cabinet. That has required a daily forty-five-minute commute each way to the Capitol. My wife, Nancy, works near where we currently live, so if we were to move to the capital city, she would have to do a daily commute. I am willing to make that ninety-minute sacrifice for a few years in order to serve the people of Utah.

With my new commuting experience, however, I have found ways to be productive with my driving time by listening to books on tape. I also occasionally ride the train and get a lot of work done during the commute. There are ways, I have discovered, to make commuting time somewhat productive.

The desire to *do* was instilled in me at an early age and has stuck with me throughout my life. Sometimes it drives my wife crazy because she enjoys sitting down to relax after a long day at work. I can't do that. I am constantly trying to figure out how to squeeze something out of each minute.

Action is a key to purposeful living. A saying I have adopted in my life to remind myself the importance of doing goes like this: "The smallest good deed is far greater than the grandest intention."[7]

That attitude has stuck with me as I have grown older. We don't have to slow down just because we are aging. If there is one quote that summarizes how I feel about living an active life, this would be it: "Life is not a journey to the grave with the intention of arriving safely in a pretty, well-preserved body, but rather to skid in broadside, thoroughly used up, totally worn out, and proclaiming, 'Wow, what a ride!'"[8]

NOTES

1. Henry Wadsworth Longfellow, "A Psalm of Life," *Voices in the Night*, 1839.

2. A. C. Nielson, "A2/M2 Three Screen Report, 1st Quarter," 2009.

3. Reader's Digest Association, "The Day We Flew the Kites," *The 30th Anniversary Reader's Digest Reader: A Selection of Memorable Articles Published by the Reader's Digest During the Past Thirty Years*, 1951.

4. John Augustus Shedd, *Salt from My Attic* (Portland, ME: The Mosher Press, 1928).

5. Henry Wadsworth Longfellow, "A Psalm of Life."

6. Robert J. Hastings, "The Station," accessed September 29, 2015, www.robertjhastings.net.

7. Quote is attributed to several people, most commonly John Burroughs and Jacques-Joseph Duguet. Some claim it is a Japanese proverb.

8. Hunter S. Thompson, *The Proud Highway: Saga of a Desperate Southern Gentleman* (New York City: Ballantine Books, 1998).

cultivate meaningful relationships

THE MAN WHO LIVES BY HIMSELF AND FOR HIMSELF IS APT TO BE CORRUPTED BY THE COMPANY HE KEEPS.[1]
—CHARLES HENRY PARKHURST

Human beings are social creatures. We are all unique individuals living our lives, but we have a basic need to associate and interact with others.

I dare say that much of the deep, lasting happiness we experience in this life will come from our relationships with family and friends. To love and be loved is one of our most basic needs. The famous psychologist, Abraham Maslow, in his 1954 book *Motivation and Personality*, listed love and belonging as one of the five fundamental needs of human beings.[2]

We all have different levels of interaction with others. But regardless of whether we interact with hundreds of people a day or only an infant child or spouse, we need to feel closeness to other human beings. Loneliness is the antithesis of joy, happiness, and fulfillment.

One of my favorite movies is *Cast Away* with Tom Hanks. Stuck on a deserted island for several years, he nearly goes mad from the solitude. Were it not for his "relationship" with the volleyball, Wilson, and the memory of his girlfriend, he would have given up on life or gone insane. The need to get back to civilization, where he could enjoy association with other humans drove him to risk his life on a flimsy raft in the Pacific Ocean.[3]

I concur with the saying, "No man is an island."[4] No one lives life in a vacuum. Nearly every day, we associate with other human beings in some capacity. How we choose to interact with them plays a key role in how happy and fulfilled we are in our lives and how much good we can do in the world.

Harvard University conducted a seventy-five-year longitudinal study of 268 physically and mentally healthy Harvard sophomores from the classes of 1939–44. These were male subjects and all white Americans. At least every two years, the men were evaluated by questionnaires, interviews, and information from doctors. The study looked at their mental and physical health, the enjoyment of their careers, retirement experience, and marital quality.

George Vaillant directed the study for more than thirty years and wrote a book about the study's findings. After all those years of surveys and interviews, Vaillant concluded that the study's most important finding is that "the only thing that matters in life is relationships."[5]

WE BECOME LIKE THOSE WITH WHOM WE ASSOCIATE

I have heard it said that we are the average of the five people we associate with most often. We tend to become like those with whom we spend the most time. If we spend time with intelligent, well-rounded people, we will most likely strive to become more intelligent ourselves. If we hang out with a rough crowd, we will tend to adopt their bad behaviors and habits.

I once was speaking with the mother of a teenager who hung out with a rough crowd, even dressing like them. She told me she was pleased that although her son spent time with friends who did drugs, her son did not use drugs himself. I kindly explained to the mother that, despite what her son told her, he undoubtedly was using drugs. She was not pleased with my assessment and probably didn't believe me. But a couple of weeks later, the police showed up at their house and arrested the young man for possession of drugs.

The simple truth is the people with whom we associate help define, in large part, who we are and how much we enjoy life. A well-known Japanese proverb states: "When the character of a man is not clear, look at his friends." So let's take a look at the most critical relationships we have in our lives and how they impact our happiness.

PARENT-CHILD RELATIONSHIPS

The greatest blessing a person can have in life is to be born into a home with a loving mother and father. Study after study has shown that children born into intact families with a father and mother have huge advantages over those who don't enjoy that upbringing. Children raised in that ideal family setting tend to, on average, have higher academic achievement, have better emotional health; have fewer behavioral problems, be less likely to become sexually active as teens, have stable and healthy romantic relationships as adults, and be more religious in adulthood.[6]

In the aforementioned Harvard Grant study, they looked at the effect of a man's childhood on his future prospects in life. The study looked at the home atmosphere, the boy's relationship with his father and mother, and whether the boy was close to at least one sibling.

The study concluded that "for good or ill, the effects of childhood last a long time."[7] And, in fact, a warm childhood proved a much stronger predictor of many aspects of a man's flourishing later in life, including his overall contentment in his late seventies, than either his parents' social class or his own income.

Vaillant, the study's director, classified those men with the warmest childhoods as "the Cherished" and those with the least-warm childhoods as "the Loveless." The result after many years?

- The Cherished made 50 percent more money than the Loveless.

- The Cherished were five times more likely to enjoy rich friendships and warm social supports at age seventy.

- The Loveless were 3.5 times more likely to be diagnosed as mentally ill (which includes serious depression, abuse of drugs and alcohol, and need for extended psychiatric care).

- The Loveless were five times more likely to be unusually anxious.

- The Loveless took more prescription drugs of all kinds and were twice as likely to seek medical attention for minor physical complaints.

Further, the Grant study found that "abundant familial love, when coupled with an emphasis on autonomy and initiative, actually produced the most stoical [able to keep a stiff upper lip] and independent men."[8]

⚷━➤

A couple of decades ago, Folgers Coffee ran a TV commercial that caught my attention. I don't often look to coffee commercials to find wisdom about life, but this commercial shared a profound truth in a simple way. It stated, "Life is about big people helping little people to be big people someday."

Indeed, parenting is a difficult job, with a primary objective of helping children grow up to be responsible adults and citizens and, hopefully, successful parents themselves.

I was fortunate to be born to loving and caring parents. I was the fourth of nine children and the only boy with seven sisters for the first ten years of my life. Our family was far from perfect, but the love of our parents overshadowed all the other family flaws. We were poor, and we went without many material things. For much of my youth, we didn't have television or a telephone, and occasionally we had no gas for heating water or running the furnace in our house. I wore my share of hand-me-down clothes from my older twin cousins, which I was always thrilled to have.

Our family likes to tease my youngest brother about a story my mother enjoyed telling. When he was in elementary school, IZOD shirts were the rage among the cool students. The IZOD logo, an alligator, was typically displayed on the chest of the shirts. One day, my brother was bemoaning our family's poverty to my mother and, with all the concern an eight-year-old could muster, exclaimed, "We're so poor I will *never* have a shirt with an *alligator* on it!"

He was right. There were no IZOD shirts in the Hale house. Yet despite all the material things we lacked in our home, we enjoyed a wonderful relationship with our parents. That is not to say we didn't have our share of disagreements and even occasional donnybrooks. As teenagers, we knew we had *all* the answers and were convinced our parents didn't have a clue about the real world. Through it all, our parents persevered with patience and continued to consistently teach us the values we needed to be successful in life.

Our parents were our friends, but they were parents first. They gave us rules and expectations. When we disobeyed, there were consequences. When we did well, there was praise. But always there was love.

Fathers Have a Profound Impact on Our Lives

Because our family was so large, our parents didn't have many opportunities to do one-on-one activities with the children. However, because I was the lone boy in the family for the early part of my life, I was able to join my father on many fun activities. He took me turkey and deer hunting and fishing in the mountains of eastern Arizona before I began grade school. I used to accompany him on sales trips throughout northeastern Arizona. He would have me join him outside by the woodpile, where we would chop wood to make a roaring fire in the fireplace. He would frequently come to watch my Little League games and would occasionally play catch with me in the backyard.

There is something wonderful and magical about a father and son who have a tight relationship. My father once told me a true story he had heard that I later shared with Pat Williams, senior vice president of the NBA's Orlando Magic and a popular motivational speaker. He was writing a book, *Coaching Your Kids to be Leaders,* and asked if I knew of any stories about teaching youth leadership principles. I sent along the story my father told me, and he included it in his book.

A high school team from a small town won the state championship game. After the game, several players got together to celebrate in an inappropriate fashion. The next day, news of what they had done spread quickly throughout the town.

There was one young man on the team who didn't participate in the celebration. He was concerned because his father was a leader in the church, and he was worried that his father would think he had been involved. All day at school he worried, and he couldn't wait to get home to tell his father that he was innocent and had not been a participant in the bad behavior.

When the young man arrived home, he dashed inside to find his father. When they met, the son didn't even get a chance to speak. The father surprised him by embracing his son and saying, "I heard about what happened at the party after the game. I just wish you had been there."

The son was astonished.

"Why?" he asked.

"Because," the father said, "if you had been there, you would not have allowed those boys to do those things."

I love that story because it teaches valuable lessons about the father-son relationship. First, the father knew and trusted his son so completely that he was absolutely confident his son wouldn't have taken part in the event. The father didn't even have to ask, "Son, were you there?" To this dad, such a thing was unthinkable. Second, the father trusted his son's leadership ability and character so much that he was confident that, had his son been there, he would have put a stop to the inappropriate behavior.

Contrast that story with the one of a father rebuking his son for not being as successful in his endeavors as he wanted him to be. To make his point, the father asked, haughtily, "Do you know what I was doing when I was your age?"

Quietly, and with bowed head, the boy responded, "No. But I know what Abraham Lincoln was doing when he was your age."

The Harvard Grant Study revealed that men who lacked a positive relationship with their fathers were "much more likely to call themselves pessimists and to report having trouble letting others get close."[9] Also of note, "it was not the men with poor mothering but the ones with poor fathering who were significantly more likely to have poor marriages over their lifetimes."[10]

Perhaps one of the most interesting results of the study was that a man's relationship with his father significantly predicted his overall life satisfaction at age seventy-five.

It is fascinating how supposed little things can have a dramatic impact on a parent-child relationship. We never know how our interaction, especially in times of stress or anger, will influence our future feelings for and about each other. Imagine how damaging to the relationship it would have been if the father with the athlete son had lashed out at his son and chastised him before learning the facts about his involvement in the party.

My daughter, Rachel, enjoys telling the story that I think helped define our father-daughter relationship. She was approaching sixteen years of age and was excited to learn to drive. My wife let her practice driving a couple of times in a safe setting.

One evening, I was with her and agreed to let her drive home. She did very well behind the wheel. As we drove up the driveway and into the garage, however, I was concerned that she was too close to the side and might hit the mirror against the side wall. I said something with an urgent tone to get her to move over to the left a little. Unfortunately, my comment flustered her, and she hit the gas instead of the brake.

We stored all our bikes in the garage in front of where we parked the car, so this story has both good news and bad news. The good news was that the bikes slowed the car's momentum before it hit the back of the garage and made a hole in the wall. The bad news was that most of the bikes were destroyed by the car running over them.

In the moment immediately after the crash, I sensed my daughter was panicking and getting upset. I, too, was rather perturbed, but I decided not to "let her have it." Rather, I made a deliberate choice to start laughing. My laughter caught my daughter off guard and defused a very emotional situation. I am certain she expected me to get angry and say or do something both of us would most likely regret. To this day, I am thankful I kept my wits about me and chose to laugh instead of lash out. That incident, I am confident, brought us closer together and showed that our relationship could transcend stressful situations.

Not long ago, I heard a story that had a big impression on me. I was speaking with Lane Beattie,[11] president and CEO of the Salt Lake Chamber of Commerce. For several years, Lane served as president of the Utah State Senate. During that time, he also served as president of the national organization for Senate presidents. That leadership position had taken him to Washington, D.C., for meetings.

After his meetings, Lane was hurrying to the airport so he could get home in time to see his daughter's recital. On his way to the airport, he received a phone call from the White House. "Lane," the person said, "the president (Ronald Reagan at the time) would like to invite you to the Oval Office. Are you available to come over and meet with him right now?"

Imagine the dilemma! Lane had an invitation to meet with the president of the United States in the Oval Office. But he also had an appointment to attend his daughter's recital.

Which would you choose? Lane chose the recital.

As he was telling me the story, he commented that he still has never been in the Oval Office and likely won't ever get there. But my guess is that, given the opportunity, he would make the same decision again. I have incredible respect for a father who would choose a daughter's recital over a visit with the president of the United States in the Oval Office.

The key ingredient in developing any relationship is time. That is especially true with parents. People like to talk about quality versus quantity time. My belief is that it takes both. It is difficult for parents to get to know their children without spending time with them. That is especially true the older the child becomes. There are no shortcuts a person can take to establish relationships, either with children or others.

Parents also need to understand they can't buy a relationship with their children. All the toys and video games in the world won't draw children closer unless there is time involved with the parent.

VAL HALE

On one occasion, I was asked to speak in church on Father's Day about parent-child relationships. I had prepared a fictional account of a son's relationship with his father over the years that I hoped would communicate how important it is for parents to make memories with their children.

Dad, I have a friend named Johnny. And he has a neat dad. He's rich 'cause he works a lot. And he buys Johnny lots of toys. He gave him a new video game the other day 'cause Johnny promised not to bother him while he was reading the newspaper after work. Dad, I promise not to make you play catch with me every night after work if you'll buy me a video game. And I won't ask you to jump on the trampoline either. Will you, Dad? Please? Johnny's so lucky 'cause he got a video game.

Dad, I have a friend named Charley. His dad is awesome. He drives a real hot car. It's a BMW. They make 'em in Germany. Charley says it costs lots of money and it's real fast. Dad, how come our car is so ugly and so slow? Why do people laugh when we drive by? Why can't we buy a BMW? Charley always tells me he wishes his dad would take him to a football game. Maybe if we sold them our season tickets, we could afford to buy a nice car. Boy, Charley's lucky. His dad drives a BMW.

Dad, I have a friend named Tammy. Her dad is a good gardener. When I go over to her house, the lawn is always plush and smooth like carpet. The flowers are so bright and lovely, and they smell so fresh. How come our lawn is always brown and trampled? And, while I'm getting these things off my chest, the only things I ever see in our flowerbeds are footprints. Dad, it's embarrassing to bring Tammy over here. She must think we're slobs. I mean we ought to quit playing those Saturday afternoon baseball games on the lawn. And those kick-the-can games at night are a lot of fun, but they're a flower's worst enemy. And Dad, I'll give you back the two dollars I won from you at the golf course yesterday if you promise to buy a gardening book with it. Tammy's sure lucky. Her lawn's green all summer.

Dear Dad, I have a roommate named Fred. He's a great guy. And his dad's even greater. Picture this. He sends Fred a credit card the other day and tells him not to worry about the balance. All the shopkeepers in town have voted Fred "Most Likely to Make Them Rich." And every girl on campus follows Fred around, begging to ride in his new Porsche. Dad, with my good looks and Fred's dad's money, the

26

women of the world would be in big trouble. Of course, so would I. It would be downright dangerous having the looks of Paul Newman and the money of J. Paul Getty. Naturally, I'd be able to adapt somehow. Hey, I have a great idea. Why don't you quit coming to see me on the weekends and send me the money you'd save? Whaddya say? Fred's dad never comes, and he lives lots closer to this place than you do. I can live without the early-morning fishing trips and the golf outings. And we could save a lot of money if we didn't go out to eat at those pizza places every time you come. Then I could enjoy Fred's lifestyle. He's lucky. His dad has a huge checking account.

Dear Dad. I love you. Why did you leave us so soon? I had hoped you could play catch with my kids after work and bounce them on the trampoline. I wanted you to go to the ballgames with us and yell at the refs like you always did. I wish my children could play just one mid-night game of kick-the-can with you and make shambles of the flower garden. And who's going to teach them to read a downhill putt or show them the difference between a rainbow trout and a cutthroat? Dad, I would give anything to have you knock on their apartment door when they're at college and kidnap them to the nearest campus pizza parlor. But I guess that's my job now. Thanks, Dad. You didn't give me video games or fancy cars or green lawns or blank checks. I was luckier than that. You gave me memories.

At the age of thirty-three, I was called to be an ecclesiastical leader of about one hundred and twenty-five families. It was an overwhelming responsibility for me, especially because there were a number of elderly people over whom I had stewardship. I decided to make weekly visits to the homes of these good, elderly citizens.

During one such visit to the home of an elderly couple, we were talking with the husband, whose deteriorating health had left him incapacitated for several years. The man, at times, had an abrasive personality that scared others away before they could get to know him well enough to discover his kind heart.

He recounted for us how he had spent his youth moving from one difficult job to another trying to make ends meet during the Great Depression. For most of his life, he had labored in coal mines, steel mills, and a variety of difficult construction jobs. I could tell he was proud of the hard work he had rendered, although his serious health problems were a direct result of work-related accidents and hazards.

As we talked further, he told of how he had decided to become a fruit farmer. He purchased some acreage and began experimenting with several varieties of fruit trees. Among his crops were peaches, cherries, apples, and pears. We listened intently as he shared his farming stories and explained the challenges of raising fruit during the mid-1900s.

He smiled as he spoke, and I saw in his eyes the satisfaction of a man who was proud of his accomplishments in life, humble though they were by the world's standards.

Finally, he finished speaking and stared out the window, reliving the memories—both good and bad—of his years as a farmer. I hated to interrupt his thoughts, but after a few moments, I asked, "What did you enjoy raising most?"

His answer caught me totally by surprise and made me laugh.

"My children!" he responded quite matter-of-factly.

The spark that had surfaced in his eyes while remembering his working days intensified as he spoke of his wonderful children. This, I could tell, was his favorite subject—his life's passion.

I still chuckle when I think of that good man's unexpected answer to my question. And yet I marvel at its profoundness. We spend much of our time in life endeavoring to raise things. We try to raise money, expectations, crops, and green lawns. Sometimes we even raise eyebrows and Cain. But the number one priority in our lives—and the fruit that should give us the most enjoyment, as this man so simply pointed out—is our children.

Relationships with Mothers Are Vital

One of the reasons most of us tend to have a strong relationship with our mother is that we recognize she has invested so much in our lives. Not only did she endure nine months of discomfort while she was pregnant with us, followed by a trip through the "valley of the shadow of death" to give birth, but she also endured endless messy diapers, throw up, tantrums, and more while we were growing up. The older we get, the more we understand the sacrifices our mothers made to raise us. We can see the unconditional love they so frequently displayed. Because they give so much love, they are easy to love in return.

One of the most famous quotes by Abraham Lincoln was his declaration that, "All that I am or hope to be I owe to my angel Mother."[12] That sentiment is shared by millions of people in the world.

I had an angel mother as well. She was an intelligent woman, though she never attended college. She was valedictorian in her high school class and was married to my father (her teacher) in May before her graduation. He had served in World War II and was ten years older than she was when they married. She had a tremendous capacity to love each of her nine children, and she made huge sacrifices for her family. I think of George Bailey's selfless attitude in *It's a Wonderful Life* when I think of my mother. She was always sacrificing her own wants and desires to make the world better for those in her family.

In our small town, there were movies shown Wednesday through Saturday in the movie theater. There wasn't a whole lot to do in the community at night, so the movies were a popular diversion. Our family couldn't afford to go to the movies very often, so my mother accepted an ushering job at the theater several nights a week, which allowed her children to attend the movies free. Some of my favorite childhood memories were in that theater watching 1960s movies like *Mary Poppins*, *The Dirty Dozen*, and *The Sound of Music*.

She was PTA president and room mother and launched six different campaigns for student government—four of which resulted in victories. She would have been a baseball umpire if she thought it would make her children happy and successful.

I remember coming home from grade school each day, bursting through the front door and yelling at the top of my lungs, "Mom! Look what I brung home from school today!"

Then I would wait for my words to echo throughout the house and for the reply that always followed: "*Brought*! It's, 'Look what I *brought* home from school. There's no such word as *brung*.'"

Having heard my mother's voice, and knowing all was well with the world, I went about my playing.

My mother had a difficult lot in life. But in spite of her challenges, she raised nine children in such a way that we all deeply felt her love and influence. Our family's financial situation made it difficult to keep the children clothed and fed. But she always managed. She was there when we needed to talk about something or have help with homework or a science fair project. I am sure she wanted to spend more time with us doing fun things, but that wasn't possible, so she did the best she could. Like many (most?) mothers, she felt inadequate when comparing herself to mothers who were more glamorous and wore nicer clothes and raised well-behaved children. But to us she was and is the world's best mother.

When I finally left home to serve a two-year church mission at age nineteen, I missed my mother terribly. I didn't fully realize how wonderful she was until I wasn't able to have her by my side. The first Sunday I was gone, I penned a poem for her to try to express my appreciation for all she had done for me.

Mommy Was Your Name

It seems like only yesterday that Mommy was your name.
But now that years have gone their way, things are not the same.
The little boy that you once knew, who loved to run and play
Has, oh so slowly, grown into the young man he is today.
The many times you combed his hair and cleaned his dirty ears;
The many nights that you were there to silence all his fears;
The many meals—his favorite kind—nice and steaming hot
Will always linger in his mind and never be forgot.
The many times you prayed with him and told him God was there;
The many times you played with him and taught him how to care;
The many times you counseled him on how to treat a girl
He'll always keep inside his heart and treasure like a pearl.
Now, Mommies leave and Moms arrive, but change they never can.
It's just that they have changed the life of a boy who's now a man.

Years later, when I was a parent and more fully realized the sacrifices my mother had made for me, I wrote her a letter on Mother's Day. I share it here because I believe it shows how important my mother's relationship was in developing my character.

Dear Mother:

Somewhere stored way back among the foggy memories of my teenage years are those incredibly painful episodes when you would exert your motherly authority and force me to do something I didn't want to do. Piano lessons, yard work, dishes, family activities, etc., come to mind. I think I even argued more than a time or two about going to a church-related activity. My repeated protests and tantrums were met with The Universal Mother's Statement, good for most any situation where a mother is forcing a child to do something against his/her will. You would look at me with pity and say, "Someday you'll thank me."

I suppose today is that day.

I want to thank you for introducing me to so many miserable things when I was growing up. Looking back, I'm glad we didn't have a dishwashing machine. As much as I hated doing dishes, I'm grateful that I had to endure my evening of washing, rinsing, drying and putting away all those dishes. And I shan't forget the yard work. I know I never set any Guinness Book of World Records keeping the lawn and yard in tip-top shape, but I'm glad that you harped on me to do as much as I did. It would probably have been easier for you to do the work yourself than to prod me into doing it. But you persevered, and I learned a little about the value of work. You encouraged, nagged, harped and goaded until I at least made an effort to do many of the things you were trying to get me to do. It was no consolation that you told me that someday I would thank you.

But today is that day.

I could have had no better mother in this world. You did so many wonderful things for me and for my siblings. Your life and service to the family were nothing short of miraculous. I didn't know of all the trials you were going through at the time, but I knew things were quite often difficult. How you put such incredible meals on the table and made sure our needs were always met, I'll never know. Given the choice of trading childhoods and families with anyone, I wouldn't even consider it. My upbringing was perfect. I was given a healthy dose of love, showered with daily gospel teachings, and attached to a long tether that gave me plenty of freedom and individual responsibility. Being part of a large, loving family such as ours was an experience I wish everyone in this world could have. As a teenager, I often saw other kids misbehaving and would think to myself: If these kids had parents like mine, they wouldn't be doing this.

I could go on and on telling you what a great mother you were/ are. But suffice it to say that I love you very much and will always be grateful to Heavenly Father for sending me to your home. There could be not greater blessing than that.

Mother, I love you very much. Have a wonderful Mother's Day!

When the Grant study looked at the subjects' relationships with their mothers, they found that a warm relationship with mothers was associated with the following:

- effectiveness at work
- maximum late-life income

- military rank at the end of World War II

- inclusion in Who's Who

- IQ in college

- verbal test scores

- class rank in college

- mental competence at age eighty

Especially interesting was that "a poor relationship with his mother was very significantly, and very surprisingly, associated with dementia." In fact, men who lacked a warm relationship with their mothers were three times more likely to get dementia in their old age.[13]

The parent-child relationship should be one of life's top priorities and most prized possessions. For many, this relationship is the source of tremendous joy and happiness or significant stress and frustration. We should work to make it the former. Nothing we do in life matters more than cultivating a great relationship with our children. That is where we will have the greatest impact on future generations. I once heard someone state that the evidence of what kind of parent we have been will be more manifest in our grandchildren than in our children.

SPOUSAL RELATIONSHIPS HAVE A HUGE IMPACT ON OUR HAPPINESS

I referred in the book's introduction to the saying, "Happy is the man who has found his worship, his wife, and his work and loves all three." Indeed, I firmly believe that the biggest and most important decision we make in our life—that which will have the greatest bearing on our happiness—will be whom we choose to marry. The second biggest decision impacting our happiness is how we choose to treat him or her.

We spend more time with our spouse (or at least we should) than with any other person. Our partner will be with us "in sickness and health." He or she will experience with us life's highs and lows. We will partner in the bearing and raising of our children. This person will be the grandfather or grandmother of our grandchildren, and it will be her or his name engraved on the headstone next to ours once our earthly sojourn has ended.

As I now look back over thirty-six years of marriage, I can honestly say that the quote rings true. There is nothing in this life that has a greater impact on our happiness—or lack thereof—than our spouses. Fortunately for me, I married one of the world's most amazing women. Her love for me and our family knows no bounds, and my love for her is profound. That is not to say our relationship has not had challenges. It has had plenty. In fact, it is working through and overcoming those challenges that has ultimately made our relationship stronger and sweeter.

My wife's grandfather understood that every marriage faces challenges, and those challenges can actually enhance the relationship. In his ecclesiastical role, he was asked to perform many marriage ceremonies. As he would counsel the couples during the ceremony, he would always say to them, "May your relationship have just enough clouds to create a spectacular sunset."

I guess that goes along with the joke that marriage is like a three-ring circus. There's the engagement ring and the wedding ring—followed by the suffering.

Our spouse, in large measure, can play a significant role in determining our success in life, including in the workplace. If he or she is supportive of our goals and encourages us to become our best selves, it is much easier to accomplish lofty goals.

I learned this firsthand. I have had some demanding, time-consuming, high-profile jobs and service opportunities, but my wife, Nancy, has always been supportive and encouraging, even when it placed a hardship on her.

In 1991, I was working as assistant athletic director at Brigham Young University. I was thirty-four years old. Ty Detmer, BYU's quarterback, had won the Heisman Trophy as the best player in college football in America the year before. The president of the Downtown Athletic Club, the organization that sponsors and keeps the Heisman Trophy, was in Provo to make a special presentation to Ty at the halftime of a BYU football game. The president of the club at the time was a successful, prominent businessman from New Jersey.

My wife and I were asked to take him and one of his associates from the club to dinner the night before the game. We enjoyed a fun evening talking about work, football, and our lives in general. As the evening wore down, this successful businessman looked at me and, in a serious voice, said, "Val, you are going to be BYU's athletic director someday."

His comment caught me off guard, and I responded by laughing nervously.

The man then pointed to my wife and said, "And it will be because of her."

I understood well what he was telling me. While I had the skills and knowledge that might someday qualify me to be an athletic director at a major university, having a supportive, intelligent, won't-settle-for-anything-less-than-the-best wife would be the difference maker for me. Her influence on me would push me to accomplish significant things. Eight years later, the man's prediction came true, and I became BYU's athletic director.

It goes back to the saying that we are the average of the five people with whom we associate most often. No one has a bigger impact on our life than our spouse. Who better to push us to become our best self and live purposefully than the person we spend the most time with?

There is no doubt my wife has inspired me to be a better person than I would have otherwise been. And I like to think I have been able to help her become a better person as well. I have supported and encouraged her in her professional goals and tried to push her outside her comfort zone whenever possible—a place where she does not typically like to go on her own.

Sometimes my "encouraging" may have gone too far. For example, I tried for thirty years to get her to take up golf. I love golf and longed for the opportunity to spend some time playing the sport with her. She, however, is a perfectionist and did not have the patience nor the desire to take up such a difficult sport. She felt like she should be able to walk out on the course and shoot even par without any practice or effort. When that didn't happen, she would get extremely frustrated and give up.

So for many years I argued and pled with her to give golf a legitimate try. Just a few lessons, I implored, and she would pick it up and enjoy it. We even got into several arguments over the subject.

Finally, Nancy relented. She reluctantly agreed to let me give her lessons. I taught her a few fundamentals but knew that having me teach her would not be a good idea. So I reached out to my friend, Todd Miller, who happens to be the son of golfing legend Johnny Miller and an assistant golf coach at Brigham Young University. Todd has a calm demeanor, and I knew Nancy would get along well with him.

After two lessons, Nancy was starting to get the hang of golf. Like all new golfers, she hit a few good shots, followed by plenty of bad shots. But the good shots were becoming more frequent.

I will never forget the evening later that summer when we played nine holes and were walking the last hole in the twilight. Nancy was anxious to finish the final hole before dark because she was playing exceptionally well. She had been keeping score in her head and realized she could shoot forty-eight if she somehow parred the last hole. It would be the first time she had broken fifty—a monumental occasion for any new golfer.

She ended up bogeying the hole and shooting a forty-nine. It was fulfilling for me to see the smile on her face as she walked off that last green having done something she never thought she could accomplish.

Nancy will never play competitive golf and will rarely play with anyone but me. But we enjoy playing an occasional round together. And I must confess that she has beaten me, an alleged five-handicapper, straight up on a couple of occasions. I always tell her that if she took the sport seriously, she would be very good.

Several times throughout our marriage, I encouraged my wife to pursue a master's degree in education. She is a good teacher, having taught elementary education and served as a teacher and instructional coach for twenty-six years. Many of her coworkers encouraged her to get a master's degree so she could become a principal. She would always tell them (and me) that she had no desire to be a principal because then she would have to deal with adult problems.

While I was serving as a vice president at Utah Valley State College, the institution transitioned to Utah Valley University and decided to add its first master's degree. The degree it chose was Education. The university had an excellent undergraduate education program, and I knew the master's program would be exceptional as well.

I was excited to learn that the degree would not be in administration but rather in curriculum. I shared the news with my wife and encouraged her to sign up for the program. Curriculum is her love and passion.

I must confess to being a little surprised when she agreed to do it. She was, after all, old enough to be the mother of most of the other students with whom she would study. She was the first person to officially apply for the program. Then she became the first person to complete all the requirements for her degree, essentially becoming the first master's degree recipient in the school's history.

The most enjoyable part for me was observing how much fun she had learning new things. Her only reason for going through the program was to learn more about the teaching profession. It was very fulfilling to see her do something challenging that she absolutely loved and excelled at.

In my relationship with my wife, and as I have counseled others over the years, I have noticed a few basic keys to a fulfilling and long-lasting relationship. These are easy to identify and talk about but difficult to achieve. However, those who are able to act on them are much more likely to find the deep joy and satisfaction that can come from a successful marriage. Incidentally, they also apply to virtually every other relationship as well.

Unselfishness

The first key to a successful marriage is unselfishness. In other words, we must put our spouse's needs above our own at all times. If the top priority of both husband and wife is to assure that the other is happy and his or her needs are being met, they are almost guaranteed a happy relationship.

The problem in many relationships arises when one or both partners start "keeping score." In other words, they keep track of how many times their spouse has done, or not done, something compared to the number of times they have done it. Scorekeeping is manifest by statements such as, "You have played tennis with your girlfriends the last two weekends, and I have had to stay with the kids." Or, "I have done the dishes every night this week. It's your turn." Or, "Isn't it about your turn to _____?" (Fill in the blank.)

There is no doubt that one of the main ingredients of unselfishness is sacrifice. In fact, sacrifice and love go hand in hand. We love those things for which we sacrifice.

In 1984, my wife was expecting our third child. The pregnancy had been hard on her emotionally. One of the things she had really missed for the first two babies was a microwave oven so she could warm up bottles in the middle of the night without having to put them on the stove to warm up. Back then, microwaves weren't as popular as they are now. They had just come onto the market not long before, and they were still fairly expensive.

I desperately wanted to get a microwave for Nancy, but I knew we could not afford one. Nevertheless, I determined to surprise her with a microwave on Christmas morning. (The baby was due in January.) Since Nancy controlled the money and the accounting in the family, there was no way I could purchase a microwave and surprise her, so I came up with a plan. I decided to skip lunch and set aside the money I would have spent for lunch each day. Over the course of several months, I could save a couple hundred dollars.

It took a great deal of sacrifice on my part to skip those lunches. I was a skinny man with a voracious appetite back then, and it took some serious self-discipline to make it happen. But I stuck with it. The sacrifice was well worth seeing Nancy's expression on Christmas morning when she opened her present and found a microwave oven. Indeed, it was the most wonderful gift I have ever given in my life. And the interesting thing was that my love for Nancy had grown because of the sacrifice I made. Every time I skipped lunch, I thought of my wonderful wife and how happy she would be with the new appliance.

Whenever my wife is asked about a favorite gift she has received, she always mentions the microwave. She understood how difficult it was for me to go without meals so she could have this badly needed appliance.

Effective Communication

One of the biggest challenges of most relationships is the lack of communication between spouses. That communication deficiency usually results from one or both spouses not listening closely to the other. And when I say closely, I mean with empathy.

I confess to being a less-than-stellar communicator in our marriage, despite that fact that both my college degrees (bachelor's and master's) are in communication. Part of the reason is because I too often try to multitask while listening, and that simply doesn't work. Frequently, my wife will be talking to me when I get home from work, and rather than looking at her and listening intently to what she is saying, I will be reading the newspaper or doing something else. I may nod my head and pretend to be listening, but my mind is frequently somewhere else.

On the other hand, my wife is a very good listener. She always remembers the things I say to her and can always tell when something is bothering me. She justifiably gets frustrated with my lack of complete attention when we talk, but she rarely makes a big deal about it. Occasionally, she will chastise me and tell me I need to listen better. Then I vow to be better and really make an effort for a while, until I lazily fall back into my old ways.

One of the keys to good communication between spouses is to make sure the timing and setting are right for a good exchange of thoughts and ideas. For example, it is not always smart to start a conversation in bed when one of the spouses is tired and hardly able to stay awake.

If there is something extremely important that needs to be said, it may not be a bad idea to come right out and say, "I have something I need you to listen to. Do you mind giving me your complete attention for a minute?" That will get your spouse's attention. It may even be worth going to a location where you can have uninterrupted conversation.

The longer a couple is married, the easier it is to "read" the others' emotions and nonverbal cues. I can tell the minute I walk in the door if something is eating at my wife. If I ask her what is wrong and she responds, "Nothing!" then I know I had better tread softly.

Men and women are wired differently, literally. In fact, brain size and structure differ in men and women. That may explain why most people (and scientists) believe women are better listeners than men.

The biggest complaint I have heard women make about men is that they just don't listen and pay attention to what they are saying and aren't attentive to their needs. Men, on the other hand, frequently complain that women expect them to be mind readers. Women, men claim, won't just come out and say what they are thinking. Women get frustrated when men don't do what they want them to do, and men get frustrated when women won't tell them what they want them to do.

Many times, communication breakdowns cause moments of distress in a relationship. Sometimes humor is a good way to defuse those tense moments. I recall the joke about the man and wife who were arguing about relatives. The man said to his wife, "No, I don't hate your relatives. In fact, I like your mother-in-law much better than mine!"

Forgiveness

A wise friend of mine once said, "A great marriage is made up of the pairing of two forgivers."

Indeed, couples that are slow to judge and quick to forgive will find their relationships much more satisfying and fulfilling than a relationship filled with blaming, contention, and finger pointing.

Forgiveness requires humility. Many times in a marriage, we feel as if we are right and our spouse is wrong. Or we feel we have been wronged in some way. Naturally, we want to defend ourselves and our position. It is hard to admit that we are wrong and our spouse is right.

Comedian Milton Berle used to joke, "A good wife always forgives her husband when she's wrong."[14]

I once heard a profound question that we should all remember to ask ourselves from time to time in our relationships. What has caused more heartache in the world: people forgetting things they should have remembered, or people remembering things they should have forgotten?

Like most people, I have done more than my share of forgetting things I should have remembered—things like names, birthdays, anniversaries, and meetings. Except for an occasional scolding or embarrassment, forgetting those things was rather harmless.

When we remember something that should have been forgotten—or forgiven—it's called a grudge. And grudges seldom result in anything good, especially in a family or a marriage.

Think back on history to people who chose to forgive and forget in their families instead of remember and seek revenge. Maybe one of the most dramatic examples of such a situation would be that of Joseph who was sold as a slave into Egypt by his brothers and suffered all kinds of affliction before being made Pharaoh's right-hand man. What would have happened if the story had gone like this?

"And Joseph's ten brethren went down to buy corn in Egypt . . . for the famine was in the land of Canaan. And Joseph was governor over the land, and he it was that sold to all the people of the land; and Joseph's brethren came, and bowed down themselves before him with their faces to the earth.

"And Joseph saw his brethren and knew them and remembered the great wrongs they had done unto him. Yea, he remembered how they had removed his coat of many colors and had thrown him into a pit. Yea, he remembered how they had sold him to the Ishmaelites for 20 pieces of silver. And his anger was kindled, and he was wroth with them. And he commanded that his older brethren, Rueben and Judah, be slain by the sword. And the others he commanded be thrown into the dungeon, where they died after many days." (Based on Genesis 42)

How history would have been altered if Joseph had not chosen to forgive his brethren of the great wrong they had committed against him!

FRIENDS AND FAMILY

Every day, when we leave our house, we encounter other human beings. It starts when we are children and continues through adulthood. The way we choose to interact with other people will have a big impact on how fulfilling our life is.

People respond differently to being around others. I am the type of person who likes to interact with others. I would probably classify myself as a social person. My wife, on the other hand, does not enjoy spending a lot of time in public. She would rather be at home with her children and grandchildren.

Nothing impacts our lives more when we are young than our friends. As a parent, I wanted more than anything for my children to have good friends who treated each other with respect and had values and morals similar to ours.

When my children were young, I would pray for their safety and success every day. As they became teenagers, I realized that even more important than praying for them was praying for their friends because I knew if their friends stayed out of trouble, my children would follow suit.

The same holds true in adulthood. The friends we have can have a huge influence on our happiness and fulfillment. They can inspire us to be better or they can drag us down. Most of us have had both types of friends throughout our lives.

About twenty-five years ago, my wife joined a group of twelve women, mainly schoolteachers, who got together once a month to play bunko and socialize. There was some turnover during the first few years, but eventually a core group of twelve women became regulars. The women range in age from thirty-five to seventy.

Initially, the group was into the game and winning and having fun. Many years later, bunko itself has taken a backseat to socializing. The ladies have become best friends.

Over the years, they have celebrated weddings and births of their children and grandchildren. They have supported each other through serious illness and the deaths of loved ones. These ladies have rallied around each other in good times and bad. When they attend bunko today, they are there to support each other and share each others' lives. Instead of writing *bunko* on her monthly calendar, one of the ladies writes *therapy*.

Our siblings can also be a source of great strength in our lives. Ever since my wife and I married, we have always gone over to my parents' home on Sunday evenings to visit. Most of my siblings also came over so we could talk about current events, sports, family, and politics. Those Sunday get-togethers have always been something I looked forward to.

When my parents passed away, I wasn't certain if the tradition would continue. But fortunately it has. My sister now owns the house, and several of us still gather on Sunday evenings to shoot the breeze and catch up on each other's lives.

The Sunday after I was let go as athletic director at BYU, I was out in my backyard barbecuing when my daughter came out and told me I needed to go to the front of the house to see something.

I walked to the front porch just as a congregation of several hundred people was making its way down the street toward our house. They held signs thanking me for my service. As I looked over the large gathering, I saw friends, neighbors, work associates, and television cameras. There were people there I would never have expected to see. It was overwhelming to see such a huge show of support.

It turns out my wonderful sisters had decided that my exit from BYU had happened without a proper show of appreciation. They had quietly gone around and invited people to join the rally on Sunday afternoon so they could thank me for the twenty-two years of service I had given the university. It was one of the most humbling and gratifying things I had ever experienced to know my sisters loved me that much. I also learned throughout that whole ordeal that you don't want to mess with the Hale siblings.

I once heard a joke that focuses on the bonds of friendship.

There was a bartender who noticed a man who would come into his bar every Friday evening and order three beers. With the drinks sitting on the counter in front of him, he would slowly drink the beers one at a time and then leave. This ritual went on week after week.

Finally, the bartender's curiosity got the best of him. He approached the man and said, "Excuse me. I have been watching you for weeks, and I have noticed how each Friday evening you come in and drink three beers. Why do you do that?

The man looked up at him and then back at his beers. He was quiet for a while and then said, "When I was serving in Vietnam, I had a couple of great buddies. We did everything together. We spent every possible minute together. One night we made a pact. We swore that if we made it back from 'Nam alive, we would get together each Friday night and have a beer. If one of us didn't make it, the other two would gather and have a beer for themselves and one for the fallen comrade. If two didn't make it, the lone friend would drink a beer for himself and one for each of his buddies every Friday night.

"As you can see," continued the man, "two of my friends didn't make it back. So I come here every Friday evening to honor their memory and keep my promise."

The bartender became emotional upon hearing the story and commended the man for his loyalty and commitment to his friends and told him the beers were on him from now on.

Time passed, and the bartender would watch the veteran come into his establishment each Friday and slowly down his drinks. Then one Friday the veteran didn't show up. Neither did he come the next or the next. Several months passed, and there was no sign of him.

Finally, the veteran walked into the bar one Friday evening, went to the counter, and ordered three drinks. Everyone in the bar was watching him, for his story was by now well known by all the regulars.

The man slowly drank two of the three beers and then got up and walked out.

Everyone began looking at each other in astonishment.

The next week the same thing happened. Only two of the three beers were consumed.

When the veteran walked in the third week and drank only two of the beers, the bartender couldn't take it any more and approached the man as he was leaving the bar.

"Excuse me," he said. "I can't help but notice that you have only been drinking two beers lately instead of three. And I remember that you told me you promised your buddies you would drink a drink for each of them and one for yourself every Friday evening. So why do you only drink two beers now?"

"Oh, yeah," the veteran smiled. "You see, I joined the Mormon Church, so *I* don't drink beer anymore."

LIVE THE GOLDEN RULE

One of the keys to developing lasting, meaningful friendships and having an impact on others' lives is merely to live the Golden Rule: Do unto others as you would have them do unto you. There really is no good excuse for treating other human beings poorly.

How we treat other people can have a real impact not only on us but also on others around us. Being nice and pleasant at all times and in all circumstances, even when things aren't going the way we want, can often make a huge impact on other's lives. Being a jerk to those around us can also have an impact—negatively.

One of my childhood heroes was a football player named Paul Linford. When I got to know him personally years later, he shared with me a story about when he was being recruited to play college football. Paul was a big, strong, fast defensive lineman who played at Granite High School in Salt Lake City in the late 1960s. He was a blue-chip recruit who was being courted by several universities. Finally, he narrowed his choices to Utah and BYU.

As the time to make the decision drew nearer, Paul struggled to make a choice. He liked both schools, and he liked the coaches. At the time, the University of Utah's program was much more successful than BYU's. In fact, BYU had won only one conference championship in school history.

One day, Paul was visiting with a friend and expressed his frustration at his inability to make a decision. His friend said to him, "Why don't you call both schools and tell them you have decided to go to the other school? Then you can see how they respond. Maybe that will help you make your decision."

Paul liked that idea. He got on the phone and called BYU. The assistant coach who had been recruiting him was named LaVell Edwards. He would later become BYU's head coach and be inducted into the College Football Hall of Fame as one of the winningest coaches in college football history.

When he got Coach Edwards on the phone, Paul said, "Coach, I have decided to sign with the University of Utah."

"I am really sorry to hear that," Coach Edwards responded, obviously disappointed. "You are an amazing player, and we would have loved to have you in our program. You are going to do great things. I wish you well in your career."

Paul said he hung up the phone from that conversation feeling terrible. Coach Edwards had shown such class and was so nice that Paul felt guilty and ashamed.

But he proceeded with his plan and next called the University of

Utah coach who had recruited him. "Coach," he said, "I have decided to attend BYU."

He had barely finished saying that when the coach began berating him. "You will never play a down at BYU! You are a lousy player and are making a horrible decision." The tirade went on until Paul couldn't take it anymore.

When he finally hung up the phone, his decision had been made for him. He picked up the phone and called Coach Edwards back. "Coach," he said, "I've changed my mind. I'm coming to BYU!"

Paul went on to become a three-year starter and a three-time first-team All-Western Athletic Conference player. (That was in the day when freshmen were not allowed to play varsity sports.) He led BYU to the WAC Championship and the 1974 Fiesta Bowl, the first bowl game in the school's history. He also played for the Baltimore Colts and Green Bay Packers in the NFL.

When everything else was equal in Paul's decision making, the way the coaches responded to him in a stressful situation tipped the scales toward the coach who replied as a friend and was more concerned about Paul's welfare than his own well-being.

I subscribe to the philosophy that strangers are merely friends we haven't met yet. Whether one is a friend should not determine how we treat him or her. We should treat all people kindly, no matter what.

In 2004, I was director of men's athletics at Brigham Young University. Our football team had just defeated Notre Dame in one of the first games of the season. Optimism was high for the remainder of the season, despite a difficult schedule.

Early the next week I went into my weekly meeting with my boss and was shocked to hear him tell me that they would be holding a press conference in two hours to announce that my contract was not being renewed. They were also not renewing the contract of the women's athletic director, who had worked at the university for forty-four years. Between the two of us, we had worked sixty-six years at the school. There is a lot to the story that I will not share here, but the firing of both athletic directors became a very big news story. For several days, our dismissals dominated the headlines.

One afternoon that week, I was at home when my son walked through the front door.

"Look what I just found on the door!" he exclaimed, holding up an envelope.

We opened the envelope and found ten hundred-dollar bills, along with a note that told a story about a man who had expressed concern when bad fortune had befallen a friend and how, when standing among a group of men, he had said, "I feel sorry for this brother to the amount of five dollars. How sorry do you feel for him?"

Of course, there was a lot of commotion among my children. We had just received $1,000 from an anonymous donor(s). The kids were anxious to run out and try to find whoever was responsible for the generous gift. However, I called them into the living room to teach them a lesson.

"If you knew who left the money on the door, do you think you would treat them differently from now on?" I asked.

They looked at each other and said, "Yes. We would be nice to them because they were nice to us."

"That's what I thought," I said. "I have a suggestion. Let's not try to learn the identity of these people. They obviously wanted to remain anonymous. If we don't know who it is, then we will have to assume that anyone we meet in our daily interactions *may* have been the person who treated us kindly. Therefore, I hope we will treat every person we meet as if they were the kind soul who gave us $1,000."

My lesson continued. "You already said you would treat that person with extra kindness, so I challenge you to treat everyone with whom you come in contact as if they were the person responsible for leaving us this money."

Several years later, my son was speaking in a church meeting. I happened to be in attendance that day. He related that story and the lesson I tried to teach that day. I was glad it had made a positive impact on him and our other children.

My wife and I have been fortunate over the years to have an abundance of friends. When challenges have come our way, those friends have rallied around us and buoyed us up. Likewise, we hope we have been able to help others in their time of need. Much of the person I have become has been a result of my friends encouraging me to do my best and serving as great examples and role models. Indeed, purposeful living is nearly impossible without family and friends.

Vaillant concluded his analysis of the epic Grant study with this statement: "The seventy-five years and twenty million dollars expended on the Grant Study points . . . to a straightforward five-word conclusion: 'Happiness is love. Full stop.'"[15]

Anyone desiring to live a life that makes a difference must do so by interacting positively with others. It is impossible to change the world for the better without involving other human beings. Developing and maintaining positive relationships is the key to transforming society one person at a time.

NOTES

1. Charles Henry Parkhurst, as quoted in Martin H. Manser, *The Westminster Collection of Christian Quotations* (Louisville, KY: Westminster John Knox Press, 2001), 338.

2. Abraham H. Maslow, *Motivation and Personality* (New York City: Harper & Brothers, 1954).

3. *Cast Away*, directed by Robert Zemeckis (Santa Monica, CA: Playtone ImagineMovers and Universal City, CA: DreamWorks Pictures, 2000).

4. John Donne, "No Man Is An Island," *Meditation XVII*, 1624.

5. George E. Valliant, *Triumphs of Experience: The Men of the Harvard Grant Study* (Cambridge, MA: Belknap Press, 2012).

6. "Benefits of Family for Children and Adults," accessed September 29, 2015, http://familyfacts.org/briefs/6/benefits-of-family-for-children-and-adults.

7. George E. Valliant, *Triumphs of Experience*, 123.

8. Brett and Kate McKay, "Love is All You Need: Insights from the Longest Longitudinal Study on Men Ever Conducted," *The Art of Manliness*, accessed September 29, 2015, http://www.artofmanliness.com/2014/09/02/love-is-all-you-need-insights-from-the-longest-longitudinal-study-on-men-ever-conducted/.

9. George E. Valliant, *Triumphs of Experience*, 135.

10. Ibid, 134.

11. Personal conversation. Permission given for use in this book.

12. Josiah G. Holland, *The Life of Abraham Lincoln* (Springfield, MA: Gurdon Bill, 1866), 23.

13. Brett and Kate McKay, "Love Is All You Need."

14. Milton Berle, accessed September 29, 2015, http://www.quote-wise.com/quotes/milton-berle/a-good-wife-always-forgives-her-husband-when.

15. George Valliant, as quoted in Scott Stossel, "What Makes Us Happy, Revisited," *The Atlantic*, May 2013.

make a difference in others' lives

**IT IS EASY TO MAKE A BUCK.
IT'S TOUGH TO MAKE A DIFFERENCE.[1]**

—TOM BROKAW

I enjoy playing racquetball. It is a thinking sport as much as a physical sport. For those familiar with racquetball's rules, you know that you only score points when you are serving. In that regard, life mirrors racquetball because we only score points—make a difference—when we serve.

Life is not necessarily about scoring points, but I do agree that no life can be truly purposeful and fulfilling if it does not somehow make a difference in the world. That doesn't mean we all have to be a Mahatma Ghandi, a Mother Teresa, or a Martin Luther King Jr. However, I believe the most joy and satisfaction in life is found when we are making a positive difference in other peoples' lives.

A difference maker can be a single mother who is sacrificing to raise her children or someone in the workplace who goes above and beyond the job description to be a friend to coworkers. It can be the businessman or businesswoman who donates time or money to a charitable cause. It can be a high school student who befriends a less-than-popular student. It can be a housewife who decides to run for city council because she believes she has something to offer.

God has blessed us all with time, talents, and treasure. When we serve, it usually involves sacrificing one or all of those three things. Of course, some of us are more blessed with talents and treasure than others, but we all are given twenty-four hours in a day to do with what we choose.

Some of us are fortunate to be wealthy. Some are poor. Some of us love the jobs we have and the work we do. Others dread going to work each day because they dislike what they do or the people with whom they work. Some of us are outgoing and interact easily with people, while others are shy and reserved. Regardless of our circumstances and talents, we are all in a position to make a positive difference in the world.

Think for a moment about your life and the people who have made the biggest positive impact on you. My guess is those impactful people were those who served you in some capacity. Your parents. Your siblings. Your teachers. Your coaches. Your friends. Your roommates.

When I was a college freshman, I had a teacher named George Durrant. He had a great sense of humor and an incredible ability to remember names. The first day of class, he stood at the door and asked students their names as they filed in. Once class started, he stood at the front of the room and went around the room repeating the students' names.

I loved going to his class and soaking in the many stories and jokes he told. Among the things he taught us was how to give a memorable speech. He said, "Sometimes I'm sitting in a meeting and someone will say, 'If you'll pardon me, I would like to tell a personal experience.' I want to raise my hand and say, 'I would love you to tell a personal experience because up until now, you've been boring!'"

George's lessons were filled with interesting experiences from his life. He was able to connect them to our lives and circumstances and inspire us to be better people.

In one of George's classes, he mentioned that he had created a personal Hall of Fame. He inducted people into his Hall of Fame who had a big influence on him and made a difference in his life. That idea resonated with me, and I decided to create my own Hall of Fame using essentially the same criteria.

I would like to introduce you to a few members of the Val Hale Hall of Fame, who earned their spot by making a difference in my life or by being a great example of how to make a difference in others' lives. These people understand service and sacrifice. They don't necessarily seek attention for what they do but rather they just live their lives, and good things happen to those around them.

MEET MIKE

Mike is one of the most positive, upbeat people I know. I have never seen him upset or "down." I met Mike when I was a teenager. My sister had a friend whose husband and Mike owned a concrete-finishing business. The two men, both of whom had the first name Michael, invited me to work for them in the summer. I wish I could say they offered me the job because they knew I would be a great worker, but I am certain they made the offer because they understood the financial circumstances of our family and wanted to help me earn some money.

Anyone who has ever finished concrete can attest that it is one of the most difficult jobs imaginable. We would start early in the morning before the sun came up and would try to get as much work done as we could before the sweltering temperatures of early afternoon arrived.

It was backbreaking work. We would tear out old concrete slabs with sledge hammers and picks and, occasionally, jackhammers. We would form up new slabs and pour the concrete and then hurry to finish it before it would set up in the heat. I would say the money the Michaels made was okay but not great. It helped pay the bills and keep food on the table.

My favorite part of the job was listening to Michael P. and Michael B. (as they called each other) tell stories. They were great Christian men who lived what they believed. Michael P. was married to my sister's friend and was a seminary teacher. Michael B. (Mike) was in his late twenties and had lived a fairly dramatic life.

In the late 1960s, Mike had been drafted into the army during the Vietnam War. Unlike the draft dodgers of that day, he decided to go make the best of his situation. He became a member of the Long Range Reconnaissance Patrol (LRRP). This little-known group of men would go undercover behind enemy lines for long periods of time to spy on the enemy and obtain information that would be used by officers in formulating strategies. It was a very important and dangerous job in a difficult war.

Unfortunately, Mike witnessed some of the unspeakable atrocities that became emblazoned on the consciousness of Americans. He was a member of Charlie Company that was involved in the infamous My Lai massacre, where he witnessed women and children being shot by Americans. It must have been a horrific experience. He eventually testified against the leader of his company and helped bring to justice some of those who had committed the atrocities.

Mike never shared with me stories from that My Lai experience, although he occasionally spoke about his time in the LRRPs. He had also been a wrestler and was one of the strongest men, pound for pound, I ever knew. He was the arm wrestling champion at Brigham Young University.

I worked on and off with the Michaels for a couple of summers. They were always good to me and had a huge impact on the way I viewed life and the way I wanted to live my life. After my freshman year of college, I decided to serve a mission for The Church of Jesus Christ of Latter-day Saints. Missionaries are required to pay their own expenses while serving, so I had been saving as much money as possible to try to cover the expenses of getting ready to go (clothes, dental expenses, and so on) and then the living expenses overseas. I knew my family didn't have the resources to help, so it was up to me to save the money, although I knew I would not be able to save nearly enough to pay all the costs. All I could do was hope I could find a way to cover the shortfall.

I was eventually called to serve in Santiago, Chile. The cost of going to that mission was $125 per month. That doesn't sound like a lot of money today, but it was a pretty good chunk of change in 1976.

About the time I was preparing to leave for Chile, Mike decided to tie the knot with his sweetheart. They were very much in love, and I enjoyed observing their courtship and marriage. Mike had always lamented that his military service in Vietnam had prevented him from being able to serve as a missionary.

One day, Mike and his new bride approached me and told me they wanted to help cover the financial costs of my mission. I was flabbergasted. Here was a newlywed couple I knew would be struggling to save money to start a family and a new life together, yet they were willing to sacrifice so I could serve the mission that Michael B. never was able to. I knew arguing with them was useless. They were determined to help.

I served my two-year mission in Chile. It was an incredible, life-changing experience that refined me and gave me the confidence I had lacked in many areas. Throughout my mission, I didn't have to worry about whether there would be money in my bank account each month when I withdrew $125. I knew Mike and his wife were making the payments.

To this day, I get tears in my eyes when I think of Mike and his wonderful wife. Their sacrifice on my behalf was significant both for them and for me. The Michaels continued to work in the concrete business. Mike and his wife ended up having fourteen children and living in the same part of the city where Mike grew up. They are an amazing couple and were recently featured in a magazine as one of the happiest couples in our area.

Mike earned a spot in the Val Hale Hall of Fame because of his incredible unselfishness toward a young man in need and his willingness to sacrifice so that I would have an opportunity to experience something he had not been able to do in his life.

I once heard the story shared by James Bender in his book *How to Talk Well*[2] about a farmer who grew award-winning corn. The farmer enjoyed a bit of a dynasty with successive years of winning the blue ribbon at the state fair. One day a newspaper reporter interviewed him and discovered one of the farmer's secrets: he shared his seed corn with his neighbors.

The reporter asked how he could afford to share his best seed corn with his neighbors when they were entering corn in competition with his every year.

"Why, Sir," replied the farmer, "didn't you know? The wind picks up pollen from the ripening corn and swirls it from field to field. If my neighbors grow inferior corn, cross-pollination will steadily degrade the quality of my corn. If I am to grow good corn, I must help my neighbors grow good corn."

The farmer understood the fundamental principle that his corn could not improve unless his neighbor's corn also improved.

The story is summed up beautifully with this quote: "So it is in other dimensions of our lives. Those who choose to be at peace must help their neighbors to be at peace. Those who choose to live well must help others to live well, for the value of a life is measured by the lives it touches. And those who choose to be happy must help others to find happiness, for the welfare of each is bound up with the welfare of all."[3]

MEET LAVELL

Up until my teenage years, TV shows were often preceded by the announcement that the program was being broadcast "live and in color." We live in a high-tech age that emphasizes fast, impersonal communication like texting and email. People are forgetting how to communicate with other human beings "live and in person." Anyone wanting to make a difference in the lives of others can most easily do so when they are communicating face to face.

In my current job, I frequently talk to business leaders about the skills they are looking for in prospective employees. Over and over, I hear them say they need employees with "soft" skills. In other words, they want employees who can communicate well, solve problems and get along with their coworkers. Our schools seem to be focusing primarily on trying to teach "hard" skills like math and reading and science. Those skills are vital for the workforce, but if our up-and-coming workers cannot work with others and interact socially and creatively, they will have a difficult time retaining a job.

The name LaVell Edwards is well known to college football fans. LaVell was inducted into the College Football Hall of Fame after coaching the Brigham Young University Cougars for twenty-nine years. During that time, he became the fourth winningest coach in college football history. The pinnacle of his career came in 1984 when LaVell's team won the National Championship by going undefeated.

LaVell is also in the Val Hale Hall of Fame. But it has nothing to do with football and everything to do with the way he treats people. In my mind, LaVell was successful as a coach not because he was a genius at Xs and Os but rather because he was a master at dealing with others one on one and in group settings.

I have spent a lot of time around sports celebrities and politicians. Unfortunately, many of them have dual personalities. They have a public persona and a private persona. In public, they are friendly and funny and charming. When the TV lights turn off, however, they are too often vain and self-absorbed and sometimes downright mean.

I "played" freshman football at BYU in 1975. I put quotations around the word *played* because it is appropriate only if you use it in the most liberal sense. It would be more accurate to say I practiced each day with the team. That was when I first met Coach Edwards.

Five years later, I was hired as an intern in BYU's Sports Information Office. It was 1980, the year Jim McMahon threw the Hail Mary pass to win the Holiday Bowl against SMU and Danny Ainge made his famous length-of-the-court dash to defeat Notre Dame in the Sweet Sixteen of the NCAA Tournament.

In 1982, I began working full time in the BYU Athletic Department and had the good fortune of associating regularly with LaVell Edwards for the next eighteen years of his coaching career. In fact, I was BYU's athletic director when LaVell retired from coaching in 2000.

During all those twenty-five years of associating with Coach Edwards, I don't recall a single time he showed disrespect toward another human being. He had every reason to be snooty and aloof because, well, that's how celebrities are, but that just wasn't him.

I remember one of my first up-close-and-personal experiences with LaVell came in 1981 while I was interning in the Sports Information Office. Dave Schulthess, the sports information director, had asked me to travel with the football team to El Paso for the UTEP game. I spoke Spanish, and he wanted me to do interviews with the Spanish-speaking radio stations along the border about Jim McMahon, BYU's record-breaking quarterback, who was a leading candidate for the Heisman Trophy.

I was a rookie in every sense of the word. I had never traveled with the varsity football team before as a player or as a media relations specialist. Everything was a new experience for me on that trip.

After the game (which BYU won), LaVell went to the press box to do his post-game call-in show with BYU's play-by-play announcer, Paul James. The players and staff, meanwhile, showered and headed to the airport, where they waited in the charter airplane for LaVell to join them.

It was late at night—well after midnight—when LaVell finished his show. Naturally, he was anxious to get to the airport because over one hundred tired people were sitting in an airplane awaiting his arrival. I was driving the car and was speeding through the streets of El Paso, trying to reunite the coach with his team as quickly as possible.

In my haste and in the darkness, I didn't see a bump in the road ahead. The car went airborne as we flew across the bump. This was in the day before wearing seatbelts was routine, and neither the coach nor I was wearing one. I am pretty sure I saw LaVell's head come close to hitting the roof of the car as we flew through the air and then landed with a thud.

Here I was, a rookie sports information staffer barely out of college, and I had just sent the head football coach's head perilously close to crashing into the roof of the car. I grimaced and braced myself for some sort of rebuke.

Instead, LaVell looked at me and laughed. Then he joked, "Well, I guess you get the Dave Schulthess Lousy Driver Award!"

Another thing about LaVell that always impressed me was that the word *no* was not in his vocabulary.

Mothers would ask him to come to their son's Cub Scout den meeting and he would go. Organizations would ask him to speak at their Rubber

Chicken Banquets, and he would agree to do it if he was available. If a friend or former player passed away, he always sent his respects and attended the funeral if it didn't conflict with a critical practice or game. For most of his head-coaching career, he even did a live radio call-in show immediately after the football games so fans could call in and ask their crazy questions or rant about something they didn't like. Can you name any other Division I coach crazy enough to subject himself to that type of torture?

I have my personal theories about why LaVell treats people the way he does. First, I believe he was trained well by his parents, Philo and Addie Mae. He was the eighth of fourteen children. A person can learn valuable lessons as a member of a big family—things like not always getting what you want, needing to accommodate others' needs ahead of yours and not being able to always have the nicest of clothing and other luxuries because of a lack of family resources. There is little doubt that LaVell's low-maintenance personality was partly a result of being raised in a large farming family.

Second, I always believe LaVell is so accommodating is because of his coaching success prior to becoming BYU's head coach. A more accurate way of stating it would be LaVell's *lack* of coaching success before becoming head coach.

In his eighteen years of coaching before assuming the BYU head job in 1972, LaVell had been involved with exactly four winning football teams. He would often note that he had enjoyed precious little success as a coach before being invited to join Hal Mitchell's BYU staff in 1962. He coached at Granite High School from 1954–62 and failed to have a winning season there. He finally had his first winning season as a coach in 1965 when BYU—under the direction of Head Coach Tom Hudspeth—went 6-4 and won the school's first Western Athletic Conference championship.

When LaVell became the surprise pick to be BYU's head coach in 1972, no one envisioned he would lead BYU to a national championship twelve years later. Most BYU fans were just hopeful he would be able to string together a few winning seasons; occasionally defeat their archrival, the University of Utah; and win a conference title or two before he was replaced by another coach.

BYU football in 1972 was barely on the radar screen of most college football fans and the media. The University of Utah and Utah State University had been the dominant teams in the Beehive State up until that time. LaVell had seen firsthand what it was like to be coach of a team that no one cared about. The media were not swarming around Provo asking for interviews from the coaches and players. In fact, the Sports Information Department had to work extra hard and practically beg to get any media coverage for the Cougars at all.

Consequently, when LaVell became head coach at BYU and began to have success, he remembered what it was like when no one cared about BYU's program. He recalled the days when no media came to practice. He remembered when fans wouldn't come to games on the opening day of the deer hunt, let alone care enough to call the radio station after the game to ask a question of the coach. To his credit, he never forgot the lessons he had learned when he and his team were not popular. It is easy to be nice to people when you are struggling to make a name for yourself, but it is the sign of a truly great person who will treat all people with respect and dignity even after they have achieved success and the label of "celebrity."

Such is LaVell.

LaVell will go down in history as one of the great football coaches of all time. He will be remembered as the Father of the Forward Pass in college football. He will be acclaimed as the founder of the Quarterback Factory at BYU. But I will always look at LaVell as the boy from Orem, Utah; the eighth of fourteen children; the coach who somehow caught a break and was invited to join BYU's coaching staff when he had never had a winning record and then was appointed head coach at BYU when few people knew who he was. When his hard work paid off and he was engulfed in success, he never changed. He never forgot his roots. He was authentic through and through.

LaVell Edwards is in the Val Hale Hall of Fame not because he was one of the best football coaches of all time, but rather because he is a celebrity who remains grounded, always treats everyone with respect, and is willing to sacrifice of his precious time to serve others.

MEET SCOTT AND JESSELIE

In this day and age, we like to comment about how busy we are. When someone asks us how we are doing, a common answer is, "Busy!" We wear busyness like a badge of honor.

Too often, I hear people excuse their lack of service in the community on their being "too busy." Well, sorry, but I don't buy that. Some of the busiest people I know with incredibly time-consuming jobs are also the most prolific with their community service. They simply make serving others a top priority in their lives. I have tremendous respect for people who are willing to make the sacrifices necessary to make a difference in the community. Then there are those who rationalize about why they don't do more community service. There always seems to be a reason—an excuse.

I understand that our ability to serve changes with life's circumstances. As an empty nester, I have a much easier time serving in the community than a parent with young children. But even a parent with young children can find some way to make a difference in the community. Perhaps they could involve their children in a service project. There may be opportunities to volunteer at the school where their children attend or get involved in the PTA. My wife's involvement as a volunteer at the local elementary school eventually led to a job offer when the children were out of the house and she was ready to go back to work.

Senior citizens have a much harder time coming up with a valid excuse about not serving. They have more discretionary time on their hands. I always enjoy walking into a nonprofit organization and seeing a retired volunteer sitting at the desk. I want to go over and hug and congratulate that person.

When I was put in charge of the Utah Governor's Office of Economic Development, I immediately became part of over thirty boards of directors. State statute requires that I sit on several of the boards. Most of the rest are business-related boards that have a strong connection to our office. As you can imagine, it requires a tremendous amount of time to be engaged with those various organizations.

When I started attending the board meetings, I began to notice that Scott Anderson, president and CEO of Zions Bank in Salt Lake City, was a member of many, if not most, of the same boards I belonged to. Attending those board meetings is part of my job. Scott, on the other hand, has a pretty demanding day job that keeps him busy. I am sure his community board service is over and above what he does for his job. I know he arrives at his office early in the morning and puts in a long day at the office. His evenings and lunch hours are often consumed with service activities.

I would have to say that Scott is involved in more good causes than anyone I know, with the possible exception of his wife, Jesselie. If it is not something business or economic-development related Scott is supporting, it is nonprofits, educational institutions, the arts, or government entities. His bio on the Zions Bank website understates that he is "active in community affairs . . . and serves on a number of business and non-profit boards."[4]

Not long ago, the Salt Lake Chamber of Commerce honored Scott for his tremendous service to and influence in the community. During the tribute, one presenter told of a conversation he had with a visitor who asked why there were so many prominent men in the community named Scott Anderson. The presenter laughed and told the visitor that they were all the same man.

Not long ago I was looking at the state statute that governs one of the state advisory committees that I chair. The statute dictates that the board chairs of four key community and economic organizations serve on this advisory committee. As I went down the list of board chairs to determine who should be serving on the board with me, I noticed that Scott Anderson was serving as chair of three of those boards. Fortunately, the statute allows a designee to serve in the place of the board chair, but I was impressed that Scott had been asked to chair (simultaneously) three critical boards in the state.

Jesselie has caught the same service bug that her husband has. She has served on over a dozen boards of directors, including as a member of the Board of Trustees for both Salt Lake Community College and Westminster College. In 2013, she was appointed a member of the Utah State Board of Regents. She maintains that service is an integral part of their obligation to each other. Sometimes I wonder when they find time to be with each other and enjoy their children and grandchildren. But I am sure they are good at prioritizing their time. They have to be.

Both Scott and Jesselie have made a huge difference in the community. They don't do it so they can get accolades. That is not their style. They have resolved to become engaged and use their time, talents, and treasure to help make their community a better place.

One of their secrets to success is that they live their lives with passion. I doubt Scott or Jesselie have ever uttered the words, "I hate my life!" My guess is they are excited about what they do. That doesn't mean they don't have bad days. I am sure they do. It is just that when they are engaged in making a difference, they are usually doing what they love.

MEET COACH DELANEY

I have a special place in my heart for teachers. My father was a teacher. My father-in-law was a teacher. My wife is a teacher. Two of my sisters have been teachers. For much of my early life, I wanted to be a teacher. I suppose that was because teachers made such an impression on me.

Most of us can probably point to a teacher or a few teachers who played a big role in our development. There is something special about a teacher who is able to connect with us and inspire us to learn more and be better.

No job or calling is more purposeful than that of teacher. I consider teaching to be one of the greatest acts of service possible. That is partly because I do not know one teacher who went into the profession to become wealthy. Nearly all of the great teachers I know are teachers because they want to positively impact the lives of their students. My wife constantly reminds me that teaching is her hobby, not her job.

When we talk about teachers in our lives, it includes more than just those we have in the classroom. Our church leaders are teachers. Coaches are essentially teachers. Even our parents are teachers.

Some of the most influential people in my life were my coaches. Most of those coaches were volunteers. They weren't doing it because they were paid. And even the ones who were paid did it mainly because they loved working with youth. They did it because they wanted to see young people grow and develop.

Bill Delaney built a track dynasty at Orem High School, my alma mater. I had always loved track and field. As a young boy, my dream was to win the Olympic gold medal in the 100-meter dash. I even went so far as to build a little track and field complex around my house.

I checked out every book I could find about track and field and memorized all the medal winners in every Olympic event from 1896 to 1964. I loved reading motivational stories about great athletes like Jim Thorpe, Glenn Cunningham, Paavo Nurmi, Jesse Owens, Jim Ryan, Harrison Dillard, and others.

When I was in sixth grade, my friends would come home and play games in the neighborhood. I, on the other hand, would put on my shorts and practice track and field events.

Finally, all my practice paid off. I was the fastest boy in the sixth grade and went to a meet in Springerville to compete with kids from other schools throughout eastern Arizona. I won the blue ribbon in the 50-yard dash and the long jump, and our team won the 200-yard relay, but we, unfortunately, were disqualified because one of our runners stepped out of the lane. Despite the disappointment of the relay disqualification, I went home that evening feeling like a champion.

Three months later, our family moved to Salt Lake City, Utah.

In our new neighborhood, I didn't have a track on which to practice. However, I made friends with a boy named Keith White. Keith had an old bamboo pole and created a pole vault pit in his backyard. He put up a couple of poles with nails in them to hold up a crossbar. Then he put out some grass clippings and sawdust for a pit to land in.

We would spend hours trying to learn how to plant the pole and fly over the bar. Keith was pretty good. I wasn't. But I learned how to jump with a pole.

The next year, our family moved again. I was now in the eighth grade. When track and field came around, I was excited to try out. Somehow, I had lost my sprinter's speed. And I wasn't a great distance runner. But I could do the long jump, and I was willing to try the pole vault, even if I wasn't very good at it.

The thing I noticed about the pole vault was that it was the sexiest of the track and field events. The girls would always gather around the pole vault pit to watch. I soon learned that was both good and bad. It was great when I cleared the bar. On the other hand, it was embarrassing when I missed or had the wind knocked out of me when I landed strangely.

My ninth-grade year I pole vaulted again and actually did okay, finishing sixth in the big, district-wide track-and-field event. I think I cleared eight-feet, six-inches that year.

I was in a bit of a quandary when my sophomore year began. I wanted to play baseball, but baseball season was the same season as track and field. For me, track and field was what I really loved, so I stuck with it.

I decided to try out again as a pole-vaulter. The era of the fiberglass poles had arrived, but I wasn't big enough to bend the poles, so I was consigned to using an old aluminum pole. I faithfully went to practice and did the obligatory running and the drills. We spent a lot of time on trampolines learning body control in the air. I loved everything about the workouts except the running.

The problem came when I began competing in the meets. The starting height for the pole vault was ten feet. I had never cleared ten feet in my life. And I couldn't make it in the meets. I was always the first person eliminated from the competition. After every meet when I got home, my mother would ask how I did. I would respond, "I finished last and didn't make the starting height."

My junior year was no better. I still couldn't make the starting height. I tried using the fiberglass poles, but I was too slow and too small to bend them. I could "straight pole" okay, but I still couldn't make the starting height of ten feet.

For two straight years I had gone to practice every day and competed in the meets and, basically, had nothing to show for it other than some good friendships. I had not once cleared the starting height in a meet.

I resolved after that season that I would not try out for the track team my senior year. Instead, I would play baseball, a sport I felt I was pretty good at. I played in the summer leagues with members of the high school baseball team and was able to hold my own with them on the diamond.

Sometime after my senior year in football, I was walking down the hall at school. Up ahead in the crowd, I saw Coach Delaney walking toward me. I quickly ducked into a doorway and tried to hide. He spotted me and came walking over.

"Hale!" he said in his always-cheery voice. "Are you going to come out and practice pole vaulting with us early in the mornings?"

During winter, the track athletes, including pole-vaulters, would go down to the Fieldhouse at Brigham Young University and work out at 5:30 a.m. I wanted to diplomatically tell the coach I wasn't interested.

"Well," I said, "I don't think I am going to be on the team this year."

That was the wrong thing to say to Coach Delaney.

"Why not?" he immediately wanted to know.

"Because I am not very good," I stated. "I haven't made the starting height in a high school track meet. And besides, I think I'll play baseball."

Coach looked at me and said, "Hale, how good were you in football as a junior?"

I wasn't very good at football as a junior but had grown three inches as a senior and had done quite well, earning all-region honors as a wide receiver.

"I wasn't very good," I confessed.

"How good were you as a senior?" he asked.

"Okay, I guess."

"No. You were a star," he said. "You were one of the best players on the team."

He had me pinned up against the wall and kept talking. "I expect the same thing out of you in track and field this year. You will be a star on our team."

What could I say? I was surprised he even knew my name. And here he was telling me I would be a star on his track team, which, I might add, was always one of the best in the state.

I have always been bad at telling people no. And, yet again, I succumbed to the pressure from Coach Delaney and agreed to attend an early-morning practice to try pole vaulting once again.

I hated waking up extra early in the morning and going to BYU to practice. But I had made a commitment, and I decided to stick with it. So I made the five-mile drive to the George Albert Smith Fieldhouse on BYU's campus. The Fieldhouse had a nice running track. On the west end of the facility was a large indoor area that included a pole vault pit. Back in the days before the Risk Management Office and the NCAA prohibited outsiders from using the facility, high school athletes were able to use the vaulting facility for practice.

After warming up, it was time for the moment of truth. I picked up one of the fiberglass poles and went to the end of the runway. I didn't have a bar up on my first run-through. I still remember the feeling as I sped down the runway and planted the pole in the box. I felt a strange sensation as the pole began to bend. When it recoiled, it shot me skyward.

I lay in the big foam pit smiling. Finally, I realized, I was now heavy enough to bend the pole. No more "straight-poling" with the metal pole. I would now be able to take advantage of the physics of the fiberglass pole.

I made another run, this time with the bar up. I easily cleared it.

I put the bar up higher and made it again.

Coach Delaney came over and watched with a big smile on his face as I was experiencing this newfound ability to soar. A distance runner in college, Coach Delaney had a reputation of developing outstanding pole-vaulters over the years.

By the end of the morning, I cleared eleven-feet, six-inches. That wasn't great, but I kept reminding myself that I had never cleared ten feet previously.

A few weeks after that, the track team met to choose its captains. To my surprise, the team elected me as a cocaptain. I reminded them I had never made the starting height in a track meet, but that didn't dissuade them from making me captain.

Top: The 1975 Orem High track team after winning the BYU Invitational. I am standing in the center on the back row. On my right is Gary Crowton, who I would later hire as BYU's head football coach. Coach Delaney is in the center holding the trophy.

Bottom: Pole vaulting in the snow at the University of Utah Invitational.

I became a better vaulter as the season wore on, in large part because I had some great teammates. Gary Crowton (whom I later hired to coach BYU's football team when I was athletic director) was a much better vaulter than I. We also had a couple of younger vaulters who would go on to become exceptional vaulters when they were seniors.

During the season, I competed in many different invitationals with mixed success. The highest I cleared was thirteen feet, two inches. At the region championship, I cleared thirteen feet and ended up winning first place and qualifying for the state meet.

At the state meet, I wasn't able to put together the type of jumps I wanted. However, I was good enough to finish in third place, and our team finished runner-up.

As an aside, after I returned from my Church mission, I walked on the track team at BYU and jumped as high as fourteen feet, six inches. That wasn't high enough to raise any eyebrows or win any competitions, but I was thrilled I had been able to keep jumping for another year.

When I look back at my life, I realize how important those four or five months on the Orem High School track team were in developing my self-esteem and confidence. I went from being a failure to experiencing a great deal of success on a very good team. I realized how much confidence and trust my teammates had in me by electing me captain. I also learned a valuable lesson by being part of a team that won a region championship and battled for a state championship.

I acknowledge that none of the above things would have happened if Coach Bill Delaney had not spotted me walking down the hall one day and refused to take no for an answer. It took a great teacher and leader to recognize that I could develop into a successful athlete and to push me to reach my potential—to become a champion.

Years ago, I read the book *Sports in America* by James Michener. I was struck by a passage he wrote about playing on a championship Little League team and the impact being a champion had on him throughout his life.

"In our little world, we were champions, and from that simple fact radiated an inner confidence that has never left me. *I could never become a bum, because I was a champion. Realizing this, I was able to lift myself onto a level of existence I could not have otherwise obtained.*"[5]

My track experience had a similar impact on my life. I went from being a perennial failure to becoming a champion. I learned the valuable lessons of persistence and hard work. Those lessons have stayed with me throughout my life and have helped lead to my success. None of it would have happened were it not for Coach Delaney.

Every once in a while, I bump into Coach. My mind immediately goes back to that winter morning in the hallway. It was such a chance encounter, but it had a profound impact on my life. I will be forever grateful for his dedication as a coach of young men and a builder of champions.

MEET PAMELA

The older I get in life, the more I admire and want to be like people who dedicate their time, talents, and treasure to caring for the poor among us. Most of us living in America are hesitant to acknowledge the extent of poverty in our country and our communities. We pretend poverty and homelessness are problems for third-world countries or the inner cities of America.

Occasionally, I run into someone who really understands what it means to care for the poor and needy. I never cease to be inspired by those people and strive to be more like them. They understand the true meaning of the word *charity* and go out of their way to share love and kindness with the less fortunate. They don't rationalize about the reasons why the poor are the way they are and how they deserve their fate. They don't judge them or condemn them. They just find a way to help however they are able.

Recently, I have had the opportunity to serve on the cabinet of Utah Governor Gary Herbert. Serving as an advisor to the cabinet is Pamela Atkinson, a wonderful advocate for the homeless and poor in Utah. In fact, Pamela has served as advisor to Utah's last three governors. She is about as close to an American Mother Teresa as I know.

Pamela's story begins in London, where she grew up in a very poor family in a mouse-infested home without indoor toilets. Her father was a gambling addict and eventually left his wife and five children. Pamela took a paper route to help with the family's finances. As is common with many poor children, she was teased about her clothes and went without many things other children take for granted.

She was a smart girl and realized the key to her future lay in education. She did her homework at a library, and a friendly librarian set aside new books for her to read. Her goal was to marry a rich man so she would "never have anything to do with poor people."

After studying nursing in London, Pamela traveled to Australia and to Philadelphia before making her way to San Francisco. She finished her bachelor's degree and earned a master's degree from the University of Washington.

She married and had three children. After her marriage ended in divorce, she moved to Salt Lake City to work at LDS Hospital. It was in Salt Lake City, where, as "an ordinary person," she began to make a difference among the poor and homeless of the city.

Through sheer determination and looking out for the "least among us," Pamela began to advocate for those whose lives had taken them down desperate and discouraging paths. She didn't cast judgment. She didn't do the blame game. She didn't get caught up in ideological debates. Instead, she went to work trying to find ways to help people—one at a time.

Gradually, her moral bank account grew, as did her influence in the community. She learned how to play the political games and pushed for resources wherever she could to help the poor and homeless. She served on the State Board of Regents for Higher Education and the State School Board. She was asked to serve on prestigious corporate boards and used the money she was paid to do more good for the homeless. Whenever community leaders would talk about gathering a group of influential people together to solve critical community problems, Pamela's name was always included. Eventually, governors came calling to seek her counsel and guidance on dealing with the poor and other social issues.

I have enjoyed getting to know Pamela these last few years. She truly is legendary in her capacity to love and care for the downtrodden. She once told me that God has a tendency to give her a "nudge" when someone needs help. I happen to believe that. I also happen to believe He is able to use her as an instrument for doing good because she is always on the lookout for people to help.

The older I become, the more I realize and believe that, outside of caring for the needs of our loved ones, nothing is more important and impactful than helping those who are less fortunate. Perhaps that is because I was raised in a poor family and experienced life from the perspective of poverty. Perhaps it is because of my belief that we are all children of our Creator and that when we serve those in need, we are only helping that Being who gave us life and cares for us all.

I used to admire those who were exceptional athletes or outstanding businessmen or extra clever. Today, however, I admire those who share their time, talents, and treasure to help the less fortunate. Imagine what a great world we would live in if we all had Pamela's passion for and desire to help others, or if we would cease passing judgment on the less fortunate and do everything in our power to help them.

Pamela Atkinson is one of the most esteemed and respected citizens of the state of Utah. She is equally comfortable with governors and paupers. Her life is about as purposeful and fulfilling as it gets.

MEET R. J.

Everyone needs a mentor in life. Unfortunately, many people never have someone they can count on to help with their career and life in general. Those who are fortunate to have had a mentor, however, will attest that such a person can make all the difference as they negotiate life's interesting challenges. If you are one of those fortunate to have had a mentor in your life, you will appreciate what I have to say about this next person.

R. J. Snow was a university administrator who had a unique opportunity. He served as vice president at two rival universities and oversaw the athletic programs at both institutions. Imagine being the vice president over athletics at the University of Alabama and then going to Auburn

University to oversee athletics as a vice president there. That is, in essence, what R. J. did when he went from being a vice president at the University of Utah to being a vice president at BYU. In both roles, he oversaw the athletic programs.

I met R. J. when he came to BYU in the late 1980s. He had just returned from South Africa, where he had spent three years as a mission president for The Church of Jesus Christ of Latter-day Saints. I don't recall much about our early meetings, other than he was always cordial.

It didn't take long, however, to realize what an exceptional people-person R. J. was. He was one of those rare individuals who made everyone feel as if they were his favorite. It didn't matter if you were a student, a professor, or a star athlete, you were worthy of his attention.

For some reason, R. J. took me under his wing. At the time, I was serving as BYU's assistant athletic director for Public and Media Relations. Since R. J. oversaw the athletic program, I had opportunities to interact with him from time to time. He was a busy man, but he would invite me to sit down in his office and talk to me about my life, my family, and my job. I knew he was up to his eyeballs in work, but that didn't matter. He always had time to talk to me. I would leave those conversations feeling like I was his favorite employee. It wasn't until years later that I realized everyone he dealt with felt the same way. He just had that unique ability to relate to people.

One day he asked if I would be interested in becoming his assistant. I was surprised by the offer. He was serving as advancement vice president at the time. I was flattered by the offer, but I didn't want to leave my role in the Athletic Department. He assured me I wouldn't have to leave athletics. He was just interested in having me assist him in some of his duties related to advancement. Originally, he wanted to give me the title of assistant advancement vice president, but he found out such a title would require approval from the board of trustees, which he didn't want to hassle with. Upon further checking, he learned he could add the title of administrative assistant without needing board approval. So I inherited perhaps the longest title in University history: administrative assistant to the advancement vice president and assistant to the athletic director for media and public relations.

For the next few years, R. J. treated me like a father. My wife and I were able to do some traveling with he and his wife, Marilyn. We became great friends and admirers of theirs.

The more I got to know R. J., the more impressed I was by the way he treated those with whom he interacted. He was always attentive and interested. I always left his presence with a smile on my face and feeling better about myself. He always expressed appreciation for the work I was doing and offered frequent words of encouragement.

After a few years in the advancement VP role, R. J. was asked to oversee BYU's campus in Jerusalem for a few years. Then he was sent to Nauvoo, Illinois. I didn't see him for a long time. When he was in town, he would occasionally stop by my office and visit.

Shortly after I left BYU, R. J. and Marilyn invited Nancy and me to dinner. We had a delightful evening together catching up on old times.

That was in 2004. I ran into R. J. at the store a couple of years later, and we talked about getting together again for dinner. I promised to call and get something set up. Unfortunately, I procrastinated making the call. Not long after our encounter, I picked up the newspaper and read that R. J. had been killed in a tragic automobile accident.

Nancy and I were shocked to learn that this man who had been such a great example of befriending and mentoring was gone. His passing left a void in our lives, but his memory stays with me always as I interact with others. I confess to coming up short in that area, but it isn't because I didn't have a great teacher and mentor.

When I think of R. J. and the wonderful way he treated others—always looking for the positive and handing out compliments—I am reminded of a story a wonderful teacher of mine once shared with me:

Of Pigs and Butterflies

A Hindu sage lived in the simplicity of a cave. Knowledge of his wisdom spread throughout the land, and many came to his secluded retreat to ask the questions that perplexed their hearts and receive answers. But the sage was a short man of ugly shape and form.

His renown spread, and the king called the sage to his presence. He was an unwise, unkind ruler, accustomed to the wealth and greed of his position.

When the sage came into the presence of the king, the latter exclaimed, addressing the sage: "You are an ugly man!" The sage made no reply.

Incensed, the king repeated himself, and, addressing the sage by name, he added, "You are a pig!"

The sage bowed and made obeisance to the king, and in the most dulcet tones, said, "And thou, Oh Majesty, art a beautiful butterfly."

Puzzled, the king asked, "How is it that I call you a pig, and you, in return, reply that I am a beautiful butterfly?"

The sage, in utter wisdom, said, "To pigs, all men are pigs. To beautiful butterflies, all men are beautiful butterflies."[6]

MEET SHIRL

Our modern society is all about being wealthy, beautiful, and famous. But the fact is, many of the people who achieve success by the world's definition find themselves devoid of happiness and contentment. Perhaps that is why so many Hollywood celebrities are in drug and alcohol rehabilitation centers throughout the world. I always find it refreshing to meet someone who has lived an ordinary, humble life and done it exceptionally well. Usually those people are happy and fulfilled and don't spend their time wishing they had things they don't. They are people who live life with the purpose of being the best they can be, without fanfare.

I agree with Robert Louis Stevenson when he said, "To be truly happy is a question of how we begin and not of how we end, of what we want and not of what we have."[7]

Shirl has been a neighbor of mine for nearly thirty years. He is a retired steel worker who spends most of his time caring for the fruit trees on his property and occasionally volunteering in the local elementary school. He lives a modest life. If you search his name online, you won't find much. He doesn't have a Facebook page or a Twitter account, and he isn't on LinkedIn.

If you consider the world's metrics for success, Shirl's name won't sift to the top. However, Shirl is one of the greatest men I know. Why?

Shirl understands what it is in life that really matters and doesn't get distracted by the fool's gold of society. He is extremely humble, quiet, and shy. He is also purposeful. I have never heard him trumpet his own accomplishments. Rather, he is quick to acknowledge when others do something noteworthy.

I have given dozens of talks over the years when Shirl was in the audience. Without exception, he has always called me on the phone later that day to thank me for the talk and to tell me it was "awesome." He does the same thing when my wife or children have given talks. In fact, I am fairly certain he makes weekly calls to everyone who gives a talk to congratulate and compliment them.

When there are service opportunities, he frequently is one of the first to sign up and quietly fills the assignment without drawing attention to himself.

Whenever I think of the phrase "without guile," I think of Shirl. I doubt he is capable of saying a mean thing about anyone. He just goes about living his life with his wife, Diane, in their quiet, humble way. And yet, they live life with purpose. They are happy. They are fulfilled. And they are making a difference.

One of the most profound and inspiring compliments I ever heard paid to a human being was paid to Shirl. A man in our church congregation once stood to share a story. He was in his home and overheard his twenty-something stepson talking in the other room to some friends or siblings. This was a young man who had experienced a rough teenagehood. For a time, his life and future had teetered on the brink of disaster. His parents divorced, and, in rebellion, he made some questionable decisions and was within a whisker of heading down a disastrous path in his life.

The boy's stepfather related that he overheard the young man say to his friends, "You know the reason I never strayed fully away from what I knew to be right? It was because I didn't want to disappoint Shirl."

I am confident Shirl had never preached to the young man about not being a rebel. He may have taught him in a Sunday School class or worked with him in Scouts. I can't say for sure. Whatever the reason, this quiet, humble man's example of goodness and love, along with his ability to convey that love for this young man through his actions, had motivated the young man to deviate from his destructive course and make something of his life.

For good and bad, I have lived much of my life in the public spotlight. Some people may envy my lifestyle. I, on the other hand, wish I could be like Shirl, quietly influencing people and making a difference in the background.

NOTES

1. Tom Brokaw, "Dartmouth Commencement Address 2005," accessed September 29, 2015, https://www.dartmouth.edu/~news/releases/2005/06/12a.html.

2. James Bender, *How to Talk Well* (New York City: McGraw-Hill Book Company, Inc., 1994.)

3. "Growing Good Corn," accessed September 29, 2015, http://www.agiftofinspiration.com.au/stories/personalgrowth/Growing%20Good%20Corn.shtml.

4. "A. Scott Anderson," accessed September 29, 2015, https://www.zionsbank.com/about-zions-bank/bio-scott-anderson.jsp.

5. James A. Michener, *Sports In America* (New York City: Random House, 1976), 19, italics added.

6. Author unknown.

7. Robert Louis Stevenson, accessed September 29, 2015, https://www.goodreads.com/author/quotes/854076.Robert_Louis_Stevenson.

get active and remain active!

AN OBJECT AT REST WILL STAY AT REST, FOREVER, AS LONG AS NOTHING PUSHES OR PULLS ON IT. AN OBJECT IN MOTION WILL REMAIN IN MOTION.[1]

—SIR ISAAC NEWTON

When was the last time you wanted to do something but simply weren't able because your body wouldn't respond? Perhaps it was when you were sick. Maybe you were injured. Or perhaps you were just too tired.

We have all heard the clichéd—but true—statement, "When you have your health, you have everything." I used to think that saying was an exaggeration. But all it takes is to be ill for a couple of days with the stomach flu or something worse to realize how important good health is to your overall happiness and your ability to be effective in life. We take for granted our mobility until a sprained ankle or pulled muscle wreaks havoc on our ability to negotiate our way around the house and the workplace.

Most of us fortunate enough to live in modern countries are in a position to make choices that can lead to healthy bodies. Yet many of us—perhaps most of us—choose to avoid habits that will almost guarantee good health and strong bodies. Our society has gravitated toward convenience and ease. Life has never been easier to live, and, not coincidentally, society has never been in worse physical condition.

Living a meaningful and purposeful life is difficult if we don't have the physical ability or energy to accomplish our goals. Cultivating and maintaining good physical and mental health will allow us to do more with and make more of our lives. The simple fact is that maintaining an active lifestyle throughout our lives will help us keep our bodies fit and capable of doing more.

My father frequently brought to our home interesting men who had strange interests or hobbies. I don't know why that was the case. He was a friendly sort and made instant friendships easily. One day in 1968, when I was ten years old, he brought home a man named Bruce.

Bruce lived in Mesa, Arizona, and had invented nutrition snacks he called Cougar Crunch and Tiger Munch. It was a compressed bar consisting of ingredients like seeds, nuts, vegetables, honey, and molasses. No one would raise an eyebrow today at eating something like that. There are dozens of similar energy bars on the store shelves today. But back then the strange concoction was a novelty.

Bruce's nickname was Crunchy Munchy, and he claimed that eating Cougar Crunch would do remarkable things for your health and energy. He boasted of being able to work all day and then run prodigious distances at a rapid pace, all because of energy-laden Cougar Crunch. He was so confident in his product that he threw down a challenge to the town's residents.

Bruce stated that he would challenge anyone to an eight-mile race. Very few people were runners in that day and age. It wasn't like today where running a 10K (6.1 miles) or half-marathon (13.1 miles) is a regular occurrence for millions of runners. Back then an eight-mile race was an incredibly long way to run. I don't remember what the prize would be, but the challenge created a stir in the community.

The key was that Bruce was going to train by eating Cougar Crunch and Tiger Munch. His competitors could train on whatever food they desired. It was all about the diet.

Because exercising and running were such rare things, there weren't many takers for the race. Finally, a man named Ron came forward and agreed to accept the challenge. I remember that he worked for the power company.

His training diet of choice? Steak and hash browns.

A date was set for the race, the prerace hype began, and the entire community waited with anticipation as the two men trained via diet and workout. The race was to be held at the Snowflake Union High School track. It would be thirty-two laps around the oval.

A fairly large crowd showed up on the day of the race. It was a small town, and this type of event created some needed excitement. Everyone wanted to see if Crunchy Munchy's Cougar Crunch would, indeed, propel him to victory.

As the runners were preparing to start the race, another couple of unexpected contestants showed up. A Navajo named Mr. Benally, age thirty-eight, showed up with his nephew, eighteen-year-old Toadochene. They were from McNary, Arizona. Somehow, word of the race had reached these men, and they wanted a shot at the prize.

The runners lined up. The pistol fired. And the big race began. They circled the track time and time again. The town's sheriff, Sank Flake, threw buckets of water on them as they rounded the track. This was, after all, the middle of summer, and the contestants were undertaking a prodigious competition.

I decided I wanted to try my hand at running, so I ran along for a few laps. I would stop for a while and then join in again. I distinctly remember several of the ladies in the crowd expressing concern to my mother that I was running so far. They were convinced I was going to keel over dead from exhaustion. Their comments and my mother's pleas for caution merely motivated me to run farther.

The race's drama didn't last long. Mr. Benally jumped into the lead and never looked back. He finished with an impressive time of 48:29, averaging just over 6-minute miles. His nephew finished three minutes behind him. Ron was a distant third, and Bruce finished last, unable to complete the final lap.

I found an online story about the epic race in the archives of the *Arizona Republic* newspaper.[2] The newspaper column explained that Ron claimed to have hurt his leg the week before in a rodeo accident, and Bruce had cracked a rib in a softball collision, a fact supposedly verified by X-ray.

After Benally crossed the finish line, the media and a group of interested spectators gathered around him. A newspaper reporter pressed to know what his training diet had consisted of. What had been the food that fueled his running such a great race?

Reluctantly, he shared his secret: Fry bread. Tortillas. Beans. And strawberry soda pop!

One of the keys to living a fulfilling, productive, happy life is being in good enough physical condition to be able to serve others and go about our daily work and activities. It is tragic when our physical condition prevents us from enjoying opportunities to do good and achieving our full potential.

I don't recall ever seeing my parents work out. For that matter, I don't ever recall seeing my friends' parents work out. Before I was born, my father was a high school football and basketball coach. He loved sports, but, as we discussed in a previous chapter, he was more of a spectator rather than a participant. He understood the value of exercise and had been extremely active as a child and young man. In fact, he talked about exercise quite often, but he chose not to make it a priority as an adult. Now, in fairness to him and those of his generation, it wasn't popular or even encouraged to exercise in the 1950s, '60s, and '70s. In fact, conventional wisdom back then said doing those things could be detrimental to your health.

I once had a conversation with Clarence Robison, the legendary Brigham Young University track and field coach whose team won a national championship in 1970. He was a distance runner on the 1948 US Olympic team. He told me that during the time he was a competitive athlete, coaches discouraged their runners from doing long-distance training similar to what is done today. They believed having their athletes run more than a few miles a week would wear them out. Coach Robison told me that if an athlete back then had used today's distance training techniques, he or she would have dominated distance racing.

Likewise, as a young teenager, I was discouraged from lifting weights because it would make me "muscle bound." It wasn't until the early-to-mid-1970s that coaches began to promote weightlifting, and athletes began reaping its benefits.

Most people, including me, get caught up in the day-to-day activities of life and don't take time to care for themselves the way they should. I don't say that to be judgmental or critical. That is just the way it is.

Living an active life and keeping yourself in shape is not an easy proposition. It takes discipline and sacrifice to expend the time and energy (and sometimes resources) required to keep fit. Getting up early in the morning to work out is a hard thing to do. Walking up the stairs instead of taking the elevator is time consuming and inconvenient. Riding a bike to work instead of driving takes longer and forces you to change clothes and possibly even shower when you get to work. Getting someone to watch your small children while you run to the gym for an hour is a hassle and can be expensive. Sometimes it requires creativity to find ways to fit in a workout during the day.

It is safe to say that getting in physical shape and staying in shape is next to impossible without sacrifice. There is no way to "veg" your way to fitness. It's yet another cliché, but there is truth in the saying, "No pain, no gain."

No matter the sacrifice, it is worth the effort to keep yourself active, if not for the present, then at least for your retirement years. The way you choose to live your life before age fifty will determine how you are able to live your life after age fifty. For those who are active and maintain a level of fitness before the Big Five-Oh, there is a good chance they will be able to remain active well into their second half-century of life.

On the other hand, a person who has lived a sedentary life up to the age of fifty and allowed himself or herself to get out of good physical condition will have a difficult time reversing course and getting in good enough shape to enjoy an active lifestyle again. That's not to say it can't be done. It is just that most people don't have the motivation and desire necessary to make such a drastic lifestyle change after years of bad habits. With people living longer nowadays, they will spend more years in either failing health or good health, depending on how they have chosen to take care of their bodies in their earlier life.

BEING ACTIVE DOESN'T MEAN YOU HAVE TO RUN MARATHONS

Living an active life doesn't mean you must run marathons or lift weights every day. Being active merely means you keep moving—you keep doing physically demanding things. Perhaps you walk to work three times a week. Or you go to a yoga class weekly. I see many octogenarians strolling through the malls each day to get their workout. Any exercise—deliberate or not—is better than no exercise.

I also caution against excessive exercise. I know people who have become obsessive about their workouts. Occasionally, they work out so hard and so often they end up getting injured or even end up experiencing marital problems because they spend so much time working out. In exercise, as with most everything, there is a good, time-tested motto: "Moderation in All Things."

My wife and I have been blessed with reasonably good health, and we have chosen to be active doing things together. We ride a tandem road bike. We go hiking, snowshoeing, and backpacking. We golf together. We are both in our late fifties. Frequently, we men-

Backpacking has taken my wife and me to some spectacular places, including the Cirque of the Towers in Wyoming's Wind Rivers.

tion to each other how fun it would be to bring friends along on our adventures. Unfortunately, the number of friends our age who are in good enough shape to join us is declining rapidly.

We have a half dozen or so friends who go hiking with us and enjoy being active, but sadly, there are far too many people our age who no longer are physically capable of enjoying hiking in the outdoors or participating in semi-rigorous activities. Many of them forfeited the ability to do those things when they quit being active. Their decision has impacted how they can live and enjoy the rest of their life.

I mentioned that my father didn't exercise much while I was growing up. Well, he finally "got religion" about exercising at age eighty-two after my mother passed away. He was driving down the road and saw a sign on a gym advertising a senior citizen discount. I believe they had a free trial period for the membership, so he went inside and signed up.

On his first visit to the gym, he went to the treadmills so he could take a walk. He wasn't quite sure how to work the machine, but he climbed on and somehow got it started. Unsure how fast to make it go, he pushed the arrows until it said 10 miles per hour. Now, that may not sound very fast, but it almost amounts to sprinter speed. As the treadmill sped up, my father couldn't keep up and didn't know how to stop it.

I still chuckle at what must have been the odd sight of my octogenarian father flying across the room, catapulted by the speeding treadmill. He landed against some other machines in the room and cut his leg quite badly. If it hadn't been such a funny and embarrassing story, he might have been more upset about the accident. At least he learned a lesson about how *not* to use a treadmill. He also learned that it's never too late to start an exercise regimen—if done properly.

PHYSICAL ACTIVITY HAS MANY BENEFITS

Living a physically active life produces many benefits. Let's start with the obvious ones. Volumes of research have shown that regular exercise and physical activity are good for you. Let's discuss some of the benefits that come from exercise and some ways to make your exercise habits easier to acquire and maintain.

Exercise to Help Control Weight

Obesity is one of the biggest and most costly problems facing America today. Some estimates claim obesity costs Americans $190 billion a year[3] in additional healthcare costs. Overweight people are more likely to suffer from a variety of health problems like high blood pressure, diabetes, osteoporosis, and so on. In fact, apart from tobacco use, "there is perhaps no greater harm to the collective health in the U.S. than obesity. In the U.S. among adults under the age of 70, obesity is second only to tobacco in the number of deaths it causes each year."[4]

There is an abundance of academic evidence to support the common-sense-logic that physical activity affects your weight. The Mayo Clinic talks about the seven benefits of regular physical activity. Number one on their list is that exercise controls weight.[5]

I will address the impact of diet on obesity and general health later in this chapter. Eating properly certainly is a huge variable in the battle to keep off excess pounds. But it all begins with an active lifestyle. When we are active, we burn calories. It is difficult to lose weight and keep it off without some sort of regular physical activity.

So how much physical activity is necessary to help keep the pounds away?

Many in government and the healthcare industry recommend we spend a minimum of thirty minutes daily engaged in physical activity to reduce the risk of chronic diseases in adulthood. That threshold, however, may be insufficient for those who are struggling with weight gain and want to shed pounds. Some scientists suggest that those who are exercising thirty minutes a day and are still gaining weight may need as much as sixty minutes of exercise a day to prevent weight gain.[6]

Of course, some lucky people have high metabolism rates and naturally burn calories without doing a lot of physical activities. The day I was married, I weighed 165 pounds and stood 6 foot, 2 inches. I could eat anything and everything and did not gain one pound for the first ten years of our marriage. My metabolism burned calories as soon as food entered my body.

The older I have become, however, the slower my metabolism has been, and I have had to work harder to keep off unwanted pounds. The tall, skinny wide receiver I once was has turned into a 215-pound linebacker (without the ripped muscles). I once heard someone say that as we age, our narrow waistlines and our broad minds change places. So it appears to have been with me.

Benefits of Working Out with Others

One of the most valuable lessons I have learned about working out is that sometimes we need others to motivate and encourage us. Like most people, I find it easy to procrastinate and rationalize away the need to work out when there is no one to push me. I have a running partner who joins me two or three days a week at 5:30 in the morning. If I didn't know he was waiting outside at that early hour to run with me, I would probably stay in my warm bed and skip the workout at least half the time. The truth is, I hate running, especially by myself. But knowing my friend is there causes me to jump out of bed when my alarm goes off. We always have a lot of fun talking about sports and politics and our jobs while we are running. Together, we came up with the title for this book during one of our runs. We joke that the things we say are done so in "runner's confidence." Those interesting, engaging conversations make the run seem much shorter and more tolerable.

If you want to begin exercising, I would strongly encourage you to find someone to join you in your workout. It is so much easier having company instead of going it alone. You can hold each other accountable and work together toward accomplishing goals.

My running partner, Peter, and I once set a goal to lose some weight and decided to make it a contest with a wager. The loser had to wash the winner's car in his driveway on a Saturday afternoon wearing no shirt. We laughed and joked about it, but the sheer terror of losing the wager and having to embarrass ourselves in the neighborhood motivated us to shed pounds. Now if I could just get my partner to pay up after losing the bet!

Working out with a partner is a good thing, but working out with several people can be even better. It is much more fun sharing the pain with others. Mixing the social benefits of being around friends with the physical benefits of engaging in physical activity is a great way to exercise.

In addition to running a couple of times a week with my friend, Peter, I often work out with my wife, riding our bike regularly. In the winter, we have a group of friends who like to go snowshoeing on Saturday mornings. I always look forward to exercising with this group because the banter while we walk is always fun and entertaining and makes the hike go by faster.

No matter your choice of physical activity, you can probably find a group of people with similar interests. When I first started biking, I looked online for a riding club. I found one locally and enjoyed riding with them every Saturday morning. Sometimes as many as twenty-five to thirty people would show up for the rides. I became friends with many of them and looked forward to seeing them each week, which helped keep me motivated to ride. In the winter, when we couldn't ride, we would go on fun snowshoeing trips in the mountains with that same group. In fact, the bikers were the ones who introduced me to snowshoeing.

The biking and snowshoeing group has a tradition of climbing to the top of Mills Peak each New Year's Day. This is a grueling 12-mile round trip hike to the top of a 10,329-foot snow-covered mountain. It is toward this hike that the group gears its training each November and December. It is not only fun but also a tremendous challenge. I did the climb twice and was surprised I made it both times.

There are running groups, tennis and golf associations, and Pilate and yoga workout groups. All it takes is a little research to find others who share your love of a specific type of working out. You will develop new friends and find others to motivate you to work out and stay active.

I have a group of friends who enjoy backpacking and being in the outdoors. Three of us worked together with the Boy Scouts and decided we wanted to do a backpacking trip—sans Scouts—each year to one of the best backpacking destinations in the West.

Our first trip was to the spectacular Buckskin Gulch-Paria Canyon between Kanab, Utah, and Page, Arizona. It is one of the most beautiful slot canyons in the world. We got caught in a rainstorm and near flash flood, but we had a great time and vowed to do another trip the next year.

Each year for several years we went on a new adventure in the spring. Other people joined us, and our group grew to about ten people. These trips were to some of the most remote, difficult-to-reach places on earth, and I usually came home exhausted, beaten up, and without all my toenails. And yet I couldn't wait for the next year when we would once again find a spectacular place for my friends and I to explore.

One of the byproducts of being part of the backpacking group was that I had to work hard to get in shape to do some of the difficult hikes through remote areas of the Grand Canyon. One of my fellow backpackers and I would load

Our backpacking group went on an epic trip each year. Here we are hiking in the Grand Canyon. I am far right in the photo.

our packs with a couple of gallon jugs filled with water and climb a nearby mountain a couple of times a week just to prepare our legs and lungs for the grueling experience that lay ahead. When it was time for the actual adventure, we were ready for the intense physical demands.

Avoid Boredom by Cross Training

Another trick to making workouts easier is to break up their monotony by cross training. In other words, don't just do the same workout every day. In addition to running a couple of times a week, I occasionally throw in a tennis match, a round of golf, a bike ride, a hike in the mountains, basketball, a game of racquetball, or some other activity. Variety is the spice of life—and of exercise.

For Christmas 2006, I decided I wanted to get a road bike so I could begin training for a triathlon. I had always wanted to run a marathon, but I injured myself training for one many years before, and I decided I didn't want to subject my body to the pounding of a marathon. I had had knee surgery a few years previously and, while my knee was still relatively healthy, I didn't want to risk injuring it on a twenty-six-mile run. I could run six to ten miles without pain, but I wasn't sure I could make it twenty-six miles without causing more damage.

So instead of running a marathon, I altered my goal to compete in a triathlon before my fiftieth birthday. My ultimate goal was to turn fifty in the best physical shape of my life, and I figured a triathlon would force me to cross-train between biking, running, and swimming.

To make my goal even harder, I was probably one of the worst swimmers in history. I couldn't swim twenty yards. In order to do an Olympic-distance triathlon, I would need to swim a mile in open water, ride a bike twenty-five miles and run six miles. The bike ride and run weren't big deals for me, but the swim scared me to death.

I signed up for swim lessons at the community pool and began the arduous task of learning to glide on top of the water. It came slowly, but eventually I got to where I could make it from one end of the pool to the other. Then I could do a couple of hundred yards. Finally, I could do a half-mile and more.

I really enjoyed breaking up my workouts between the three activities. Running, biking, and swimming each use different muscles. One morning I would run five to six miles. The next I would swim laps totaling a mile. Then I would ride my bike for several hours a couple of times a week. Each day brought a new workout challenge.

I competed in the triathlon and finished in a time of two hours and twenty-six minutes, good for seventh place in my age and weight category. As you might guess, the event I did the worst in was swimming. I swam over half of the mile on my back doing the backstroke, not the ideal stroke for an open-water swim. But I didn't care. I survived the swim and went on to finish the bike and the run in respectable times. That was my primary goal. I also reached my goal of being in the best shape of my life when I turned fifty. A couple of weeks after the triathlon, I did my first century (hundred-mile) bike ride.

Use Future Events as Motivation

When I purchased my road bike, my wife expressed a desire to get one as well. We would occasionally ride together, but we would both get somewhat frustrated because I would have to ride slower than usual to allow her to stay up with me. And she would have to ride faster than usual to keep up with me. The result was that we both ended up frustrated and not enjoying the experience.

After we had been riding for a few months, we participated in a sponsored ride with some friends. One couple rode a tandem bike, while the rest of us rode our individual bikes. Afterward, my wife made the comment that she would like to try riding a tandem bike. On a tandem, I could ride as hard as I wanted, and she would be right there with me the entire time. We thought about it for a few months, and the following Christmas decided to splurge and buy a tandem.

We had heard all the jokes and stories about how tandem bikes cause divorces and magnify any problems in the relationship. But we went ahead and made the investment. Eight years later, we frequently tell others that purchasing a tandem bike was one of the best things we ever did. We have logged thousands of miles on the bike together and enjoyed each other's company while getting a good workout.

We have also learned the important lesson that the easiest way to stay committed to a regular workout schedule is to sign up for a future event or activity. For example, a good friend of mine, Jim Wall, knew of our love of bike riding and approached us about riding in the annual Seattle-to-Portland (STP) Bike Ride. It is a popular ride in the middle of July that attracts ten thousand riders. Most participants ride the 206-mile route from Seattle to Portland over two days. They spend the night at the half-way point in Centralia, Washington, and then continue on to Portland the next morning. About one-fourth of the riders, however, ride the entire route in one day. That is what Jim wanted us to do with him.

At first, I was a little reluctant about doing such a difficult ride and wasn't sure Nancy would want to join me in something that strenuous. When I asked her, however, she enthusiastically agreed to try it. With only three months before the ride, we knew we would need to get busy training to be able to make the all-day trek from Seattle to Portland.

The first thing we did was sign up for the ride. It typically sells out, so we wanted to make sure we secured a spot. The ride wasn't cheap. It cost nearly $150 apiece. The fee was nonrefundable—just the way I wanted it.

Writing the check was the equivalent of Cortes burning his boats so his men would have to either fight or die. We had made a $300 investment in the race, and that helped motivate us to train.

Next, we went online and found a training schedule that would allow us to finish the ride in one day. It required training rides of varying lengths during the week, including several rides of one hundred–plus miles. We knew we couldn't shirk the workouts if we wanted to be able to do the ride without being miserable and risk not finishing. We had to ride long enough and far enough to get both our legs and our rear ends in shape for the adventure.

We were diligent about our training regimen and headed into the double-century ride fairly confident we could finish it. Sure enough, we rode all throughout the day and pulled into Portland just as the sun was going down. We figured we were on the bike about twelve hours and twenty minutes. It was a huge accomplishment for us. We had so much fun we did it again the next year with some other friends. The second time we cut three hours off our time.

The most important lesson I learned from that experience, as well as my triathlon experience, is that your ability and desire to stick to a training schedule is greatly increased if you sign up for an event, preferably with a non-refundable deposit. We would never have ridden the number of miles we did and spent the number of hours on our bike we did if we had not committed financially and emotionally to the STP bike ride and our friends.

Nancy and I beside our tandem during the Seattle-to-Portland bike ride. We rode 206 miles that day.

Exercise Helps Your Emotional and Mental Health

I have talked a lot about the future benefits of living an active life. But more important than the future is the here and now. The main reason to work out and get in good physical shape is because it will help you live a more fulfilling life *today*. There are obvious physical benefits to your heart and muscles and body that come from being active. But just as important are the mental and emotional benefits that come from physical activity. Studies show that regular exercise promotes a positive boost in mood and lower rates of depression.[7]

Occasionally, we hear people talk about a "runner's high." This euphoric feeling is caused by endorphins and creates a positive feeling in the body similar to the drug morphine, except that endorphins are not addictive. Those who exercise regularly not only get the boost from the temporary "high" that comes from exercise, but they also enjoy the positive feelings associated with knowing their bodies are in shape. I have noticed in my own life that I tend to feel the best about myself when I am fit and in good physical condition.

My wife is a beautiful woman who weighs almost the same today as she did the day we were married. In fact, I don't think there has been a time in our marriage (except when she was pregnant) that she couldn't don her wedding gown and look just like the twenty-year-old bride I married. That said, for much of our marriage, I half-jokingly told my wife she had been "cursed" with a great body.

Why would I say that?

Because my wife didn't need to work out regularly to keep her great figure. Sure, she has been disciplined in what she eats, but for much of our marriage she hated and avoided working out, especially running. Consequently, she missed out on the significant mental and emotional benefits associated with physical activity. Being skinny does not equate to being in good physical condition.

When we both reached our fifties, Nancy agreed to start working out and doing regular strenuous physical activities with me. And for the first time, she began to experience the emotional side effects of exercise. I noticed an almost-immediate change in her emotional state. I guess the best way to describe it is she appeared to enjoy life more, and her emotional highs exceeded her emotional lows. It was obvious she was feeling better about herself both physically and mentally. There was no denying she was a different person mentally and emotionally because of the physical activity.

My daughter has always been active in sports. She was an excellent volleyball player and has been an active runner. Her fourth child was born with a chromosomal disorder that caused numerous health complications, including necessitating a tracheostomy. The baby required 24/7 care and, because of the tracheostomy, could not be left without someone who had been trained in trach care. Consequently, my daughter spent most of her days at home with her baby and her other three children. Needless to say, the demands of her family and the little baby were almost overwhelming for her.

My wife, who became certified in trach care, understood what my daughter was going through and would occasionally call her and tell her she was coming over to watch the kids so my daughter could go running. Nancy knew the time out in the fresh air running would give our daughter some badly needed exercise, but it would also help clear her mind and help her de-stress. My daughter was always extremely grateful for the opportunity to get some exercise during those difficult times.

SIGNIFICANT HEALTH BENEFITS COME FROM EATING WELL

To this point, I have touched mainly upon the physical and emotional benefits of exercise and remaining active in order to allow us to live a fulfilled life. This discussion would be incomplete, however, without some mention of the role diet plays in our overall well-being.

When you were young, you probably heard your parents or a teacher say, "You are what you eat." There may be more truth to that than we want to admit. In the United States, we have never had more options regarding what we eat each day. Unfortunately, with our lives centered on ease and convenience, much of what we consume is designed to be prepared and eaten fast. We don't care as much about the food's content as we do about how it tastes and how easy it is to fix.

The problem is that much of the "fast food" we consume is full of sugars, saturated fats, salt, preservatives, and other unhealthy ingredients. While consuming an occasional supersized hamburger, fries, and soda may not inflict too much long-term damage to your body, repeated consumption of those and other unhealthy foods may lead to obesity and other serious diseases, like type 2 diabetes.

There are hundreds of diets out there for people who want to get control of their eating habits. Some are more effective than others, especially over the long haul. I have friends who swear by a vegetarian diet. Other friends eat protein-heavy diets. I have discovered that people are passionate about their diet of choice. If it works for them, they don't want to mess with it, and they are convinced it will work for others. They almost become proselytes for their diets.

For me, the most effective thing I have found goes back to my mantra: "Moderation in all things." I have a hard time going cold turkey from eating specific types of food. Part of the reason is that I have a lot of work-related eating engagements. These aren't the types of meetings where I order food off the menu. Rather, most of these are occasions where some-one places food in front of me. I then must choose whether to eat that food or not. It isn't easy to be picky in those circumstances.

I don't eliminate anything from my diet; I just try to keep from eating too much of any one thing. I eat an occasional burger or hot dog. I try to curtail (usually unsuccessfully) the amount of dessert I eat. I drink an occasional soda or juice.

Obviously, the key to losing weight and keeping it off is to cut down the number of calories you consume, as well as maintain some type of regular exercise program. Any long-term, successful weight-reduction or maintenance program requires both of those elements.

There are two or three dietary changes we can make that will have a significant impact on our health and wellness. They are fairly simple changes, but they require a significant amount of discipline for most people.

Reduce the Size of Our Portions

We Americans eat a lot of food. We usually eat until we are full. Our mothers instructed us to eat *everything* on our plates. Sorry, mothers, but that advice may have contributed to our bad eating habits. What you should have told us is to eat until we were content. Then stop. We tend to feel guilty when there is good food remaining on our plate, but we need to get over it and walk away from the table when our hunger is satisfied.

Our tendency is to make and eat a lot of food. We eat far more than we need for our bodies and minds to remain active and healthy. Most of us could cut in half what we eat and still have plenty of calories to burn throughout the day.

I once heard a health professor explain that when he and his wife go out to eat at a restaurant, they order one entrée and split it between them. He said it usually is more than enough food to leave them content. I decided to try it and found that he was correct. My wife and I occasion-ally split an entrée when we find a menu item we both want to eat. When we do that, we usually leave the restaurant feeling better, both about eating less and having saved money by only having purchased one entrée.

If I order my own entrée, I now don't feel obligated to eat everything on the plate. Sometimes I only eat half of it and ask for a "doggie bag" to take the remainder home for another meal. That way I squeeze two meals out of one and don't stuff myself at the restaurant.

Most of the articles I have read indicate it is better to eat smaller portions of healthy food and eat more often during the day. So instead of having an unhealthy snack at work when your blood sugar gets low, try having something healthy on hand to squelch those hunger pangs. It may require that you bring something with you from home that meets your healthy nutrition goals. Fruits and vegetables are always a great snack.

Don't let yourself get too hungry during the day. When you get overly hungry, the tendency will be to overeat when you finally get some food in front of you. Eat when you are hungry, but be sure to eat healthy, nutritious food.

Avoid Sugars and Fatty Foods

Most scientists and nutritionists agree that excessive consumption of sugars and fatty foods is the primary reason for the obesity epidemic in America today. We love to eat our sweet foods. I didn't realize this until I spent a couple of years living in South America. I ate with the natives for most of that time. Their food was much more bland than ours and was made fresh with fruits and vegetables. There was essentially no such thing as creating meals from cans and boxes.

After eighteen months of eating native food, I moved into a home with a cook trained to fix American-style food. I was surprised that it took me a couple of weeks to become reaccustomed, with both my digestive system and my taste buds, to the sweeter foods we Americans regularly eat. I hadn't realized there was that much of a difference.

I have several friends who have sworn off sugar in their diets and reaped the rewards physically and mentally. For those who were consistent in their efforts, they experienced significant weight loss merely by cutting back on things like sodas and desserts.

In this day and age, soda and juices made from concentrate are the biggest sugar culprits. Nearly half of all Americans drink soda every day. And, believe it or not, the average is 2.6 glasses per day. Males age eighteen to twenty-nine are the biggest consumers. They average a half-gallon of soda per day.[8] The liquefied sugar found in sodas is more quickly absorbed into the digestive system. Caffeinated drinks are also popular nowadays, and the caffeine can be addictive, which means it can be even harder to avoid those drinks.

I confess to being one who loves juices and soft drinks. It is difficult for me to pass up a nice sweet drink when it is in front of me, especially on a hot day. There have been stretches of time where I have been able to abstain from soft drinks, but eventually I fall off the wagon. I rationalize that it is okay to drink diet drinks. While they are probably not quite as harmful as regular soft drinks, I doubt they are doing anything good for my body. A glass of water would be a much better choice. But that requires discipline, and, as I always joke with my wife, "The only thing I can't resist is temptation."

I guess, like so many others, I am a bit of a sugar addict. I love to eat sweet things. My mother was an excellent cook and had a knack for making great desserts. We didn't eat many meals that didn't include dessert. When I was first married, I joked with my wife that I would give the meals she cooked a grade, and she could not get above a B grade if the meal didn't include a dessert. Fortunately, she ignored my poor attempt at humor and helped wean me, somewhat, from regular desserts.

Don't get me wrong. We still have desserts from time to time. Sunday dinner usually includes a dessert. And I make an occasional batch of chocolate chip cookies or other treats. My wife is an outstanding chocolate maker. She dips over a thousand chocolates at Christmas, which means we have delicious chocolates sitting around our house tempting me for several weeks.

Having chocolates sitting around the house at Christmas has taught me another lesson: one of the tricks to avoiding unhealthy snacks is to not have them in the house. If there is ice cream in the freezer and I am suffering sugar withdrawals, I will probably find the ice cream and indulge myself. If there is no ice cream nor brownies nor cake, I will probably reach for an orange or apple or watermelon. Replace those sugary and fatty snacks with healthy ones in your pantries.

I admire those who sit by me at banquets and take a bite or two of their dessert and then push it aside. Meanwhile, I am finishing every last bite of my dessert and asking my neighbor if she is planning to finish hers.

The reality is that if you can control your intake of sugar and fatty foods, your health will benefit significantly. Your weight will likely decrease, and you will feel better physically and mentally. You will not experience the highs and lows that come from eating lots of sugar.

We all hope to live a happy, fulfilling, purposeful life. That is much easier to do when our bodies are functioning properly and we have good health. Occasionally, unfortunate things happen to us that are out of our control that may impact our health; yet most of us have the ability to choose whether to live a healthy lifestyle or not. For your physical and emotional well-being today and in the future, I encourage you to become active and eat healthy foods.

NOTES

1. Isaac Newton, Newton's First Law of Motion.

2. *Arizona Republic*, August 4, 1968, 41.

3. National League of Cities, "Economic Costs of Obesity," accessed September 29, 2015, http://www.healthycommunitieshealthyfuture.org/learn-the-facts/economic-costs-of-obesity/.

4. Harvard School of Public Health, "Obesity Consequences: The High Cost of Excess Weight," accessed September 29, 2015, http://www.hsph.harvard.edu/obesity-prevention-source/obesity-consequences/.

5. Mayo Clinic Staff, "Exercise: 7 benefits of regular physical activity," accessed September 29, 2015, http://www.mayoclinic.org/healthy-lifestyle/fitness/in-depth/exercise/art-20048389.

6. Heather Hatfield, "Your Exercise Routine: How Much is Enough?" WebMD, July 30, 2009, http://www.webmd.com/fitness-exercise/guide/your-exercise-routine-how-much-is-enough.

7. WebMD, "Exercise and Depression," accessed September 29, 2015, http://www.webmd.com/depression/guide/exercise-depression.

8. "Soft Drink Consumption: The Frightening Statistics and Associated Health Risks!" http://www.everyday-wisdom.com/soft-drink-consumption.html.

love your work

NEVER CONTINUE IN A JOB YOU DON'T ENJOY. IF YOU'RE HAPPY IN WHAT YOU'RE DOING, YOU'LL LIKE YOURSELF, YOU'LL HAVE INNER PEACE. AND IF YOU HAVE THAT, ALONG WITH PHYSICAL HEALTH, YOU WILL HAVE HAD MORE SUCCESS THAN YOU COULD POSSIBLY HAVE IMAGINED.[1]

—JOHNNY CARSON

My first declared major in college was accounting. After returning from my LDS mission, I did not know what I wanted to do for a living, so I asked several people I admired what major I should choose. Of course, my thinking was that my major would lead to my profession. One man, a college business professor whose opinion I greatly valued, suggested I major in accounting and go on to get an MBA.

That sounded like good advice, so I signed up for the accounting program. I took math classes, Accounting 201, and a few other prerequisite courses for the program. I did pretty well in the classes and enjoyed accounting well enough, but I kept envisioning myself spending my career behind a desk crunching numbers (or counting beans, as we used to call it), and I wasn't excited about that prospect.

Truth was, I didn't feel good about my decision to pursue an accounting and business career. So I began trying to think of another possible major that would lead to a career I would enjoy more.

My mind harkened back to my eighth-grade English class in 1970 taught by Phyllis Bestor. In that class, she introduced us to the first VCR I had ever seen. It was a big camera and recorder that could capture our images. We were fascinated by this amazing technology that allowed us to see ourselves in action, both live and recorded.

Mrs. Bestor divided the class into groups and assigned each group to make a TV ad. Our group decided to make an Ex-Lax commercial to promote the popular laxative. We spoofed a popular Nestlé chocolate ad that was running on TV at that time. The Nestlé ad had a jingle that went something like this: "N-E-S-T-L-E-S. Nestlés makes the very best chocolllllaaaattte!"

Our ad mimicked the jingle with the words: "E-X-L-A-X. Ex-Lax makes the very best chocolllllaaaatte!"

Yes, it was crude junior high humor, and the kids in the class loved it! But, more important, I enjoyed the process of creating the commercial.

Years later, as I was trying to decide what I wanted to do for a career, I kept thinking back to that eight-grade commercial and how much fun it was to make. Consequently, I made a trip to see the advisor in the communications department.

"I think I want to major in advertising," I told the advisor. She smiled at me and asked, "What do you enjoy doing?"

I thought for a minute and responded, "I like to write and be creative. And I like public speaking and photography."

The advisor nodded and said, "It sounds to me like you ought to go into public relations."

I looked at her, bewildered, and asked, "What is that?" I had never heard of public relations before she mentioned it.

"Public relations," she said, "is everything you just told me you like to do, and more."

"Okay," I responded. "Sign me up for public relations!"

And just like that my career course was set. I was going to be a public relations practitioner, even though I knew absolutely nothing about the field.

When I arrived at my first public relations class, taught by a legendary professor named Rulon Bradley, the first thing he told us was, "If you choose to go into public relations as a career, your life will go by quickly."

I thought that was an odd comment for him to make. Yet thirty-five years later, I must confess he was correct. It seems like just yesterday that Dr. Bradley made those comments. My life *has* gone by quickly. Thinking back over those years, I can't think of a single day I dreaded going to work. With one exception, I have loved the jobs I have had. The saying, "Time flies when you are having fun" is especially applicable when it comes to your job.

JOB SATISFACTION HELPS
DETERMINE YOUR HAPPINESS

When we reach the end of our lives and give an accounting of the time we spent on various activities, most of us will discover we have expended more time working than in any other activity, except possibly sleeping. Over the course of a forty-year career, the average person will have spent more than eighty-three thousand hours on the job.

It is difficult to live a purposeful and happy life if you dread going to work each day or feel as if your job is inconsequential. Granted, not everyone is going to love his or her job. But having a job that is meaningful and challenging and pays a decent wage can contribute significantly to self-fulfillment.

More and more today, young people are choosing jobs that not only take care of their financial needs but also make a difference in the world and match up with their passions. The popular term used to describe this career approach is purposeful employment or the purpose economy.

Unlike our fathers' era, today's workers rarely stay with the same job for their entire lives. A new study in *The Atlantic* suggests that jumping between jobs during a person's twenties has been shown to improve chances of higher work satisfaction and higher pay in their thirties and forties.[2] That is both good news and bad. The good news is that if we don't particularly like a job, there is a good chance we can move on and find an even better opportunity. The bad news is that, in times of economic uncertainty like today, finding a great job can be difficult for many people.

So how do you find a job that is both fulfilling and challenging? My experience is that if you follow your passion, you will find a profession that is both fulfilling and fun. It may not be the first job you get or the second, but eventually a door will open to a job that you enjoy. And chances are it may not be the type of job you originally thought you would have.

Hardly a month goes by that I don't have someone call me and ask how he or she can get a job in athletic administration. They know I was once athletic director at a Division I university, and they want to know what they can do to get a similar job. Usually, they begin by telling me their job is not as fulfilling as they would like, and they love sports, so they want to know how they can transition into athletic administration.

My answer usually does not make them very happy. I explain that there are thousands of people just like them who want to break into athletic administration. That means they will likely need to find some way

93

to start at the bottom of the ladder and work their way up, one rung at a time. That is how I did it, and only rarely will someone become a top athletic administrator without previous experience working in athletics.

I once hired a man named Peter Pilling as my senior associate athletic director at BYU. Peter knew well what was required to become an athletic administrator. Like me, he had majored in accounting in college and had taken a job as an accountant in Southern California. After several years, he realized he did not want to be an accountant for the rest of his life. His passion was athletics. So Peter quit his job and applied to the sports administration master's program at Ohio University. He moved his family across the country and went back to school. Once he had his degree, he began moving around the country, working at universities like Morehead State; St. Bonaventure, Wyoming; and Villanova, all the while earning his stripes. He started on the bottom rung of the ladder and slowly worked his way up.

I hired Peter as my associate because he was not only competent professionally, but he was also passionate about working in athletics. He was willing to pay the price to advance his career, and his dedication and sacrifice eventually paid off in landing him a job at his alma mater. After leaving athletic administration for a decade, Peter got back into the profession and is now director of athletics at Columbia University in New York City.

BIG SALARY OR FUN JOB?

Early in my athletic administration career, friends would come up to me and say, "I really would like to work in athletics like you. What do I need to do to get a job in athletics?"

I would smile at them and say, "Well, first let me tell you how much money I make. Then let's see if you are still interested."

Usually, they would shake their head in disbelief when they learned about my salary and would decide that making a lot of money was more important to them than having a really fun job that did not pay much. I guess since I had never had a job that paid a lot of money, I was content with the salary I had, and I didn't view it as a sacrifice to have that job.

Sometimes if you follow your passion into a career, it may be a job that does not pay a lot of money. If that is the case, you likely will have a decision to make. Do you want to have a job that is more like a hobby (or a jobby, as some call it), or do you want a job that is less enjoyable but pays more? If you are fortunate, you will find a job that pays well and is fun and fulfilling.

When I graduated from high school, I thought I wanted to be a teacher. In fact, I wanted to be a coach. However, my father, who had been a high school coach and teacher, discouraged me from pursuing that career. He warned me that I would have a difficult time providing for my family on a teacher's salary. His repeated warnings caused me to steer clear of that profession. That is one of the reasons I have so much respect for those who choose to go into the teaching or coaching profession.

My wife has a unique philosophy about her job. As I previously mentioned, she is an award-winning teacher. She began teaching shortly after we were married and taught full time for three years. Then she opted to stay at home to raise our children for a few years. Once they were all in school, she decided to return to teaching. The catch, however, was that she did not want to teach full time. As luck would have it, the elementary school where our children attended had an opening for a part-time music and PE teacher. My wife had received a music minor in college and loved sports, so she was a natural for the job.

After teaching music and PE for five years, Nancy was approached by the principal about teaching sixth grade. She said she would do it, but only if she could teach part time. By then, Nancy had established her reputation as a great teacher, so the principal figured out a way to accommodate her request.

After Nancy had taught sixth grade for seven years, the school district approached her about becoming an instructional coach to help first-year math teachers in the junior highs. She agreed to go to the district on one condition—that she be allowed to do it part time. That was eleven years ago, and she still works part time for the district, training teachers. She also occasionally teaches as an adjunct faculty member at the local university.

For many years, I would encourage Nancy to take up a hobby of some kind. I encouraged her to try tennis or golf or something she would enjoy on a regular basis. Her response was always, "Teaching is my hobby. It's what I love." When I would ask her if she ever considered teaching full time, she always said the same thing: "As long as I am teaching part time, it is my hobby. If I have to teach full time, it will become a job."

It did not matter that she would not make as much money working part time. The truth is Nancy has always been more concerned about doing something she loves and about making a difference in the lives of students than about making a lot of money. I have often told her she would be an excellent education consultant, where she could share her teaching knowledge and ideas and parlay that into a lucrative career. Every time I mention that to her, however, I am met with a blank stare that I understand to mean, "How many times have I told you that I am not a teacher to make money? I am a teacher so I can make a difference in students' lives in the classroom."

The allure of more money and increased prestige can be tempting in our professions, justifiably so. Most of us want to "climb the ladder" professionally. Only the truly disciplined realize what their skills and limitations are and are willing to walk away from promotions and opportunities to make more money if those options do not fit their talents or their personal aspirations.

When I was in athletic administration, I watched several times as talented assistant coaches wanted desperately to become head coaches. It is only natural for any coach to want to "call his own timeouts." Yet there were some assistant coaches who I knew would not make good head coaches. They were brilliant as assistants but likely would not fare well as head coaches for a variety of reasons, usually because they did not have the organizational, leadership, or people skills needed to be successful as a head coach.

The late Doug Scovil was a perfect example of a football coach who was an offensive genius and brilliant offensive coordinator but didn't make it as a head coach. In the late 1970s, Doug installed an innovative passing attack in LaVell Edwards's offense at BYU and revolutionized the game of college football in the process. The media called him Air Scovil, and he churned out record-setting BYU quarterbacks like Gifford Nielsen, Jim McMahon, and Marc Wilson. BYU consistently led the nation in offensive production and broke dozens of NCAA records while Scovil called the plays.

Doug left BYU after the 1980 season to become the head coach at San Diego State. Everyone expected the Aztecs to become instantly successful under Scovil's magic. There were billboards throughout San Diego promoting Scovil's inaugural SDSU season that proclaimed, "The Pass is Back in the Aztec Attack!"

Unfortunately, Scovil's offensive genius did not translate into success as a head coach. He developed some very good players and had a prolific offense, but the Aztecs did not have a defense to match, and Scovil was fired after the 1985 season. He returned to the National Football League and enjoyed success again as an offensive assistant coach until he passed away unexpectedly from a heart attack in 1989.

Doug's story is repeated over and over again in the athletic realm. Coaches who are great at calling plays and overseeing an offense or a defense are promoted to head coach, only to be fired a few seasons later.

The same thing regularly happens in businesses and other organizations. Someone is successful as a salesperson or worker, and the boss asks him or her to become a manager. Success in one area, however, does not always translate into success in another realm. I have often talked to people who, after being promoted to a "higher" office, said, "I wish I had my old job back. I enjoyed it so much more than this one."

The point is that more responsibility and more pay does not always equate to more happiness and fulfillment. Sometimes it does, but often it results in more stress and headaches. It is like Charlie Bates told me when I was first married: "The more money I have made, the more problems I have had to deal with." Simply put, there may be times when you should consider where your talents and abilities are best utilized and be content to serve in that role. Other times you should stretch your wings and move outside your comfort zone as you attempt new professional challenges.

The popular author, lecturer, and Harvard professor, Clayton Christensen, explains in his book, *How Will You Measure Your Life?* that too often we give up on our dream of finding a job that is challenging and fulfilling. He talks about how many times we end up doing something professionally that is completely different from the path we started down. In his case, he always dreamed of being an editor for the *Wall Street Journal*. That was his dream job. However, through a series of twists and turns, he ended up as a professor at the Harvard Business School and discovered that teaching college students was his true "dream" job and calling in life.[3]

I can certainly relate to what Christiansen says. The day I graduated from college, my goal was to become a public relations practitioner in the international division of a Fortune 500 company. That is what I had worked toward for most of my college career. I had interviewed with Dow Chemical to work in their Latin America division and had made it to the final two candidates but was beat out by a native Panamanian who had a degree in PR and a minor in chemistry.

I graduated from college in 1981 at a time when the economy was suffering in America, and jobs were scarce. I sent out a lot of résumés and looked high and low for a job, even if it wasn't in public relations. I was married and had a little baby, so I needed money to keep food on the table.

After a few months of job searching with no success, I applied to be a reporter for the local newspaper. I had done well in my journalism classes and had even been named "Reporter of the Term" while writing for the school paper. I did not particularly like the idea of being a news reporter, but I figured it would look good on my résumé as I searched for a better PR job. I accepted the job and began working for less than $1,000 a month, which was even less than my wife was making as a first-year teacher.

It turns out that being a newspaper reporter was the one job in my career I did not enjoy. I did not mind meeting people and writing stories. What I despised about the job was the "need" to include controversy in my stories, especially if there was none to be found. On one occasion, my editor handed me back a story I had turned in to him and said, "Get some controversy in this story, or no one will read it."

"There is no controversy," I responded. "It's a pretty straightforward story with no conflict."

The editor glared at me and said, "Then no one is going to read it. The readers want controversy!"

After that exchange, I knew my days as a reporter were numbered, and I sped up my job search. Luckily, timing was on my side. During the time I had been working as a reporter, BYU had been expanding its football stadium from thirty thousand to sixty-five thousand seats. There was talk that they might hire a full-time marketing person who could help put fans in the stands of the massive new facility.

I had previously worked as an intern in the Sports Information Office under Dave Schulthess, and he had been mentioning my name as a candidate to fill the new position. He wouldn't be the one making the hire, but he would have some say in the process. The other key players in the decision were athletic director Glen Tuckett and Scott Williams, director of special events. Scott had the most say in whom the new hire would be because the person would report to him.

I was excited because the job was right up my alley. I would be marketing athletics and other special events, in addition to producing publications for the athletic department. The job combined my love of advertising and marketing with my public relations skills.

I survived the interview process and was thrilled beyond description when they offered me the job. I would actually get paid to do my hobby every day. It wasn't a lot of money, but it was certainly more than I had been making as a newspaper reporter, and I couldn't have chosen a more fun profession.

About a year later, I received a call from Dow Chemical telling me they had a job for me if I was still interested. I had a decision to make. Did I want to return to the international PR path that I had originally started down? It would be more lucrative and would probably take me out of my comfort zone and be challenging. I had spent most of my college experience training for that type of job. The alternative was to continue doing what I was doing and see where it led me. I loved my job and was living close to my family and my wife's family.

I chose the latter and have never once regretted it.

For twenty-two years I worked at BYU, moving up the ladder from one job to the next. I went from marketing and promotions to fundraising to becoming the assistant athletic director for external relations to the athletic director.

Honestly, I never envisioned myself working anywhere but BYU. But then came that fateful day when, during a regularly scheduled meeting, my boss informed me they would be holding a press conference in two hours to announce I would no longer be athletic director. It was a huge, unexpected shock to me, and it put me in the position of trying to figure out what I would do for the rest of my career. Had BYU chosen to handle the situation differently, I may have had a future in athletic administration. But I knew that athletic directors who are fired have a difficult time being picked up by other universities, so I was pretty much forced to find another field in which to work.

I decided to visit with several friends who had been successful in their careers and ask them what they would choose to do if they woke up one morning and learned they no longer had a job. Their responses were very interesting. Almost without exception, they mentioned that they would pursue an opportunity that had something to do with their passion in life. One friend, a successful advertising executive, told me he would open a restaurant because he loved cooking and had always wanted to do that.

I had multiple job offers come my way shortly after the news broke that I would be leaving BYU. A friend of mine who was head of a multi-billion-dollar company told me not to accept any offers until I had spoken to him. I flew to meet with him at his company headquarters, and he asked me to be his personal public relations manager, as well as head up public relations for his company. The salary he offered me was a great deal more than I had been making. It was a tempting offer, but I just couldn't get comfortable with it for a number of personal reasons.

A few months previously, while playing tennis, I had been introduced to William Sederburg, president of Utah Valley State College. UVSC was a large four-year college located in Orem, Utah, where I lived. President Sederburg and I had played a couple of tennis matches together and were becoming friends. I decided to call Bill and ask to meet with him.

When I walked into Bill's office, he was accompanied by his chief assistant, Cameron Martin, a good friend who I had gotten to know at BYU many years previously. One of his vice presidents, Val Peterson, who later became one of my closest friends, was also present.

I walked into the room not quite knowing what to expect. When we sat down, President Sederburg turned to me and said, "Val, what would you like to do at UVSC?"

His question caught me off guard. I guess I had not thought much about that. I responded, half joking: "I always said in my next life I would be a university professor."

"Oh," he replied, "You don't want to be a professor. Have you ever considered being a lobbyist or doing community relations?"

I explained that my formal training was in public relations, so community relations would be something I would be comfortable with. However, I had never done lobbying, although I felt I could become pretty good at it.

I probably need to set the stage for this discussion. A few weeks previous to my meeting with President Sederburg, the college had become embroiled in a controversy that had become national in scope. The student body officers had invited filmmaker Michael Moore to speak at UVSC only a couple of months before the 2004 presidential election. Moore had produced several controversial films critical of the war in Iraq and was an outspoken critic of President George W. Bush.

Utah Valley, home of UVSC, is one of the most conservative counties in America. Many members of the community, when they learned of the Michael Moore invitation, became incensed and tried doing anything they could to force UVSC to rescind the invitation. Threats were hurled at the administration in many forms. Even national commentator Sean Hannity joined the battle. In the end, the college agreed to invite Hannity to speak to "balance" out Moore's speech.

My meeting with President Sederburg was at the height of the Michael Moore brouhaha. Bill was looking to find someone to help with community relations, and the fact that a high-profile person like me might be available to fill that role was appealing to him. He could not offer me a full-time position because there was no full-time position available. However, the school had recently received a large donation from a donor to be used to help elevate the college's profile in the community. President Sederburg said he would like to hire me as a consultant until such time as a full-time position could be created.

The job sounded fun and interesting. It didn't pay as much as I had been making or had been offered by others, but it was a decent wage. UVSC was an up-and-coming institution that was on its way to becoming a university. I loved higher education, so I decided to accept President Sederburg's offer.

I worked as a consultant at UVSC for nearly a year. Then I was hired as assistant vice president for External Affairs. I oversaw community relations and served as legislative liaison for the institution, in addition to overseeing the school's economic development efforts. After a year in that role, I was hired as advancement vice president and then vice president for University Relations. One of my favorite roles was to help the school successfully transition from a college to a university and become the largest university in the state. I worked for eight years at the university and loved every minute of it.

I left Utah Valley University in 2012 to become president and CEO of the Utah Valley Chamber of Commerce. A lot of people thought I was crazy to leave UVU, and maybe I was. Nevertheless, I saw the chamber job as an opportunity to make a difference in the community and get outside my comfort zone again. I had spent thirty years in higher education, and this new job would utilize many of my skills, yet introduce me to new challenges and opportunities.

For two years, I was able to serve the business community in Utah Valley, which at the time was ranked among the best places in America to do business. I enjoyed the job immensely and envisioned myself retiring from that role. Then one day, I was with Utah's governor, Gary Herbert.

His chief of staff had resigned a couple of months previously, and I inno-
cently asked if he had found a replacement yet. He looked at me and said,
"No. Are you interested in the position?"

His question caught me completely off guard. I said, "Governor, I am
not looking for a new job. But if you want me to apply, I would be happy
to do that."

He then said, "You know, there is a job coming open soon that would
be a better fit for you than the chief of staff position." He then told me that
the executive director of the governor's office of economic development was
planning to leave in the near future and asked if I would be interested in
that role. I gave him basically the same answer as before. He responded:
"Okay. I'll put you on the short list and be in touch for an interview."

After about five interviews with the governor and others, I was offered
the job. It was overwhelming, to say the least. I tried to convey to my wife
the magnitude of the responsibility I would be undertaking. She was used
to my having high-profile jobs, so I don't think it fazed her.

It wasn't until we attended a press conference in the Gold Room of
the State Capitol, where the governor introduced me to a packed room
of media and business and community leaders that the full weight of the
job's responsibilities finally sank in. As we were driving from the Capitol
to meet with my new staff, I turned to Nancy and asked, "What do you
think?"

She looked at me, let out a sigh, and said, "This is a *big* job!"

In fact, the job has turned out to be probably the most fun and enjoyable of my career. It is an extremely busy job, but it offers me the chance to
meet almost daily with fascinating people and businesses. I am a member
of the governor's cabinet, so I meet weekly with him and his staff to discuss important issues for the state. And the team of employees I work with
are incredibly smart and capable. I couldn't ask for a better experience.

Frequently, I am asked to speak to university students. Almost always,
they ask questions about my career path. I tell them that if anyone had
told me on the day I graduated from college that I would one day become
athletic director, university vice president, chamber of commerce president, and economic advisor to the governor, I would have laughed out
loud in disbelief. Never would I have imagined myself doing those things.
Yet the stars aligned, and I was open to new opportunities when they pre-
sented themselves. The result has been that I have been fortunate to have
more than three decades of incredibly fun jobs.

LESSONS ABOUT GETTING AND KEEPING JOBS

Throughout my career, I have learned a number of valuable lessons I would like to share because they may help others find and keep jobs they love. I share these concepts frequently when I speak with students or other groups interested in employment. Again, these aren't ideas I learned from a textbook. These are things I have experienced and observed.

It Really Is WHO You Know

We have all heard the cliché: "It's not what you know but who you know." When it comes to finding a job, no truer words have been spoken. As I look back on my career, only a couple of times did I ever apply for a job. I applied to be an intern, and I applied to be a newspaper reporter. But other than that, I have gotten my other jobs because I knew people.

After working as a student intern in the Sports Information Office, my boss, Dave Schulthess, lobbied for me to become the promotions and marketing director for the athletic department. Without his intervention, I doubt I would have been hired. Once I had my foot in the door of the athletic department, it was up to me to work hard and show that I deserved promotions. Over the course of twenty-two years, I went from student intern to director of athletics.

When I left BYU, I had begun developing a friendship with Bill Sederburg at UVSC. That budding friendship certainly played a key role in my being hired there. However, just as important was my previous relationship with Cameron Martin, Sederburg's chief assistant. Martin and I had gotten to know each other years before, when Cameron was a student working in the BYU Alumni Association. We had stayed in touch through the years. I have no doubt that Cameron put a bug in Sederburg's ear that he needed to hire me to help with community relations.

When I left UVU, I was serving as chairman of the board of the Utah Valley Chamber of Commerce. I resigned my role as chair to apply for the president/CEO position when the previous president retired. I had a great relationship with members of the board of directors and the search committee, so I had an inside track to the job. Fortunately, I received the job offer, and I embarked on a new career opportunity that I thought would take me to retirement.

Governor Herbert invited me to apply for the executive director of economic development position in his cabinet because he knew and trusted me. We had become acquainted over a decade previously while he was still serving as a county commissioner and I was BYU's athletic director. We had stayed in touch over the years through our regular work interactions and by playing an occasional round of golf or a tennis match together.

In each instance, relationships were the critical factor in my getting the job. The reality is that most jobs are essentially "filled" before they are posted. Hiring someone straight off the street or from a résumé is a bit of a rarity anymore, especially in management. Therefore, it is important to develop a network of people throughout your working career. It really isn't all that difficult to meet people and get to know them. You never know when the person you met at the work reception or the Chamber of Commerce reception will one day be hiring for a position in his or her company at the same time you are on the job market.

Set Yourself Apart from Others

So what is the secret to making your name pop into the mind of an acquaintance when he or she has a job to fill?

The key is to have found a way to set yourself apart from others before a job ever comes open. In other words, in your interactions with others, you should do things that make you stand out from other people, things that demonstrate your exceptionalism.

As an example, I found that a great way to distinguish yourself from others is to send hand-written notes of congratulations or thanks. There was a time that I had a goal of writing one handwritten note each day. Sometimes I wrote them to complete strangers who I had read about in the newspaper or to a friend who had received a promotion at work. I especially wrote them to thank people who had done nice things for me.

On one occasion, I decided to write a note to a colleague I had always admired at work. I told him in the note how I had been impressed by the way he treated people and the way he went about doing his job. I thanked him for being a great example to me.

I was surprised to see my colleague's reaction when he received the note. He was genuinely overcome with emotion and couldn't thank me enough. Ever since the day I wrote that note of gratitude, we have been fast friends. He even remembers my anniversary every year and has occasionally bought dinner for my wife and me as an anniversary present.

I remember once writing a note to an executive who took me golfing on a very nice golf course. He called me when he received the note and said, "In all my years, no one has sent me a note thanking me for taking them golfing."

Yet another time I wrote a congratulatory note to an entrepreneur I barely knew whose photo was on the cover of a business magazine. Years later, after he sold his business for a handsome profit, I ran into him at a reception. I had forgotten about the note, but he reminded me of it and mentioned how impressed he had been to receive it. The fact that he remembered it years later shows what an impact it had on him.

After receiving a congratulatory note from me for receiving an award, one lady named Andrea (whom I had never met) wrote back the following: "Thank you so much for your kind letter of recognition. It was so nice to open up such a pleasant letter on a stressful day. What a surprise! What a wonderful thing it would be if we all followed your example. It reaffirmed for me the idea that small things really can make big differences. Thank you for being a great example to me!"

Another way to catch someone's attention is to do something nice for them "just because." Sending a treat to a friend at work with a note saying you are doing it just for the heck of it is a great way to make someone's day. And it will make you stand out.

I am a believer that your appearance in the workplace will have an impact on the opportunities that come your way. Granted, the dress code in the workplace is different today in some professions than it used to be. People tend to dress more casually than they did twenty years ago.

My philosophy, however, is that you should always dress for the job you want, not the job you have. In other words, if you aspire to be the manager, you should dress like a manager. The boss is going to have to project you into that role, and if he or she can't picture you as a manager, you likely won't get the job.

When I started working as a newspaper reporter, I was somewhat embarrassed by how some of my colleagues dressed. They were ultra-casual, even to the point of being sloppy. They would cover important events in their casual attire, while everyone else was in a coat and tie.

I determined I would wear a coat and tie to work every day. Some of my coworkers ribbed me about dressing up, but I felt it was important to show class. A few of the female reporters actually complimented me on the way I dressed. I knew I didn't want to be a reporter for the rest of my life so I needed to dress like a businessman in case I came in contact with a potential employer.

Whenever I speak to students, I always encourage them to stand out by dressing for the job they want to have rather than the job they currently have.

Leave Your Job in a Respectful Manner

Odds are in this day and age that you will change jobs more than once or twice. Here is something to remember that will impact your future in more ways than you would imagine.

President Matthew Holland, with whom I worked at UVU, taught me an important lesson as he was transitioning from university professor at BYU to university president at UVU: How you leave your job is just as important—if not more so—than the way you come into a job.

What did he mean by that?

When I was a teenager, there was a song with the title, "You Can Take This Job and Shove It!" I could always imagine an angry worker shouting those words at his boss with an accompanying obscene gesture and then storming out the door.

While doing something akin to that might feel good for a few minutes, chances are those antics will come back to haunt you and will close doors in your future. That boss may someday be called by a future employer to give a reference about your work and character.

When you leave a job, you should do everything possible to leave in the classiest way possible, even if you believe you have been treated poorly.

When I was let go as athletic director at Brigham Young University, there was no shortage of people who felt I had been wronged. I received dozens and dozens of letters from friends expressing anger at the treatment I had received. Letters to the editor were filled with scathing comments about my supervisors and the way a Christian university had treated both me and my colleague, Elaine Michaelis, who was also fired the same day after forty-four years of exceptional service. I suppose I had every right to be mad and lash out at those who had chosen to treat me the way they did. Nevertheless, when I got home from work that morning, my wife and I talked and prayed about the situation and decided to stay on moral high ground. We chose at that moment to not let that situation define us and dictate how we would react and feel. We chose to become better, not bitter.

In my years working in athletics, I had seen plenty of coaches come and go. Some were fired. It is almost inevitable that you will someday lose your job if you work in the athletics profession. I had witnessed some coaches leave quietly and with class, and I had seen others leave kicking and screaming and breathing threats. I had decided that if I were ever fired or asked to leave, I would do so in as classy a manner as possible. I didn't want to be like those who threw a tantrum on the way out the door. I resolved that I would learn from the experience and just move on to the next phase in my life. And I wouldn't let that negative experience leave me an unhappy person or cast a doubt on my self-worth and my abilities.

As I left my house later that afternoon, there were TV reporters on the front lawn waiting to interview me. I am sure they couldn't wait to put a microphone in my face and hope I would say something in anger that would make a great sound bite or news clip. As it turned out, I tried to be cordial and upbeat. I even cracked a few jokes. When asked what I was going to do next in my career, I joked, "Well, if I can't find any reputable work, I can always return to being a news reporter."

My response was certainly not what the reporters were expecting or hoping for. They were looking for controversy and anger. The result of the interviews, however, was that the public rallied around me and came to my defense.

To this day—more than a decade later—I regularly get people, some of them complete strangers, who approach me and say, "I have so much respect for the way you responded when your were fired by BYU. I don't think I would have been that cordial and nice about it. Thank you for the example."

In all honesty, if I had gone out kicking and screaming and threatening lawsuits and saying angry things in the media, I am convinced I would not have been offered the jobs at Utah Valley University, the Chamber of Commerce, and the governor's office. Those doors would have been closed by my actions.

Remember that when the time comes for you to leave a job, whether it is voluntarily or by compulsion, walk out the door with class. Any other way will close doors to you down the road.

Make Your Boss Look Good

In all the jobs I have had, I had one goal: Make the boss look good. When the boss looks good, the entire organization looks good, and everyone working in the organization benefits. When the boss doesn't look good, the entire organization will be affected negatively.

I always had a hard time understanding some of my coworkers who seemed to delight in criticizing and second-guessing the boss. They somehow felt their tearing him or her down and backstabbing would elevate their status. But it doesn't work like that. I didn't always agree with the things my bosses did, but I always wanted my work to make them look good.

When I worked in the Sports Information Office, my job included helping to promote various athletes for All-America honors and other special recognition. It was interesting to see how athletes responded to being promoted for these awards. Some were so concerned about receiving individual recognition that it affected their performance and the team's performance in a negative way. In their eyes, it was all about them. They demanded to know what we were doing to promote them and their accomplishments.

Fortunately, most of the athletes we worked with understood that the most important factor in their receiving individual recognition was how the team performed. If the team was winning, more attention would come to them individually. If the team was losing, they would be less likely to be singled out for individual honors. They, therefore, focused their primary attention on winning as a team.

The same thing holds true in our businesses and organizations. When the entire team is winning, it is easier to be singled out for individual accomplishment. When the team is performing poorly, individual accolades will be harder to receive. Whether you like him or her, the boss is in charge of the team, and the team's success will be a direct reflection on the boss.

I once was talking to a former BYU athlete who was a member of an NBA championship team. I made the observation that just about anyone could coach that team given the talent they had. The player laughed and then told me that sometimes when a teammate was shooting a free throw at the opposite end of the court, the coach would wave him over and tell him to stand beside him. Then he would tell him to pretend like they were talking so people would think they were actually strategizing.

I got a good laugh out of that story. That player helped make his boss look good during the games, both by helping him fool the fans and media with the appearance that he was always coaching his players and by helping him win the world championship on the court.

Living a purposeful, joyful life is much easier when we have a job we love that is making a positive difference in the world. But regardless of what your job is, you should strive to do and be the best you can. I have never known anyone who achieved personal fulfillment by being a slacker and just getting by. We should take pride in what we do and attempt to get maximum joy out of our employment. To quote an old Scottish saying: "What e're thou art, act well thy part."

NOTES

1. NLCATP, "20 Remarkable Johnny Carson Quotes," accessed September 29, 2015, http://nlcatp. org/20-remarkable-johnny-carson-quotes/.

2. Derek Thompson, "Quit Your Job," *Atlantic*, November 5, 2014, http://www.theatlantic.com/business/archive/2014/11/quit-your-job/382402/.

3. Clayton M. Christensen, Karen Dillon, and James Allworth, *How Will You Measure Your Life?* (New York City: HarperCollins Publishers, 2012), 49–52.

be a lifelong learner

INTELLECTUAL GROWTH SHOULD COMMENCE AT BIRTH AND CEASE ONLY AT DEATH.[1]

—ALBERT EINSTEIN

Monroe and Shirley Paxman are in their mid-nineties, having reached and passed the age when most people have retired to a rocking chair in a rest home. Yet unlike most folks their age, this couple is more active than many people half their age. When asked about the secret to aging so gracefully, Shirley always proclaims, "You turn off the TV and get out of the house!"

Each Monday morning, the couple sits down together, checks the calendar of events in the newspaper and begins filling out their schedule for the week. Nearly every day, they attend a lecture or a cultural event at one of the two local universities, Brigham Young University and Utah Valley University.

While working at UVU, I was surprised to see the Paxmans show up at nearly every significant guest lecture at the university. After all, this elderly couple had to fight traffic and the usual parking nightmares on a college campus and make their way through the halls to the auditorium where the lecture would be. Doing those things is daunting for anyone, let alone a couple of super-seniors. Yet week after week, lecture after lecture, there the Paxmans were, sitting on the front row, ready to learn.

Their love of learning did not just take root in the evening of their lives. This couple has spent their entire lives learning and serving. Monroe was a judge for many years. Shirley raised seven children and then went back to get her master's degree in child development and family relations. They have served their community in many capacities and raised their family in a culture of learning and serving.

Their daughter Susie once told a newspaper reporter that one of her favorite memories was having her mother come to her third-grade class to check her out of school so she could accompany siblings to a cultural event at BYU.

The Paxmans wanted to expose their children to a wide variety of cultures and experiences. They signed up to be official hosts for the US State Department for international dignitaries traveling through Utah. On several occasions, those dignitaries stayed at their home. Daughter Annette tells of a time the prime minister of Sudan was staying in their home and she accidentally came upon him praying in her bedroom, which had been assigned to him for the visit. It was a very impactful experience for her and left a lasting impression.[2]

When I think of those who live purposeful lives, I picture people who are avid and diligent learners. They have a hunger and curiosity for knowledge and information throughout their entire lives. They understand that those who quit learning quit progressing. To quit progressing is to fail to meet your potential. Failure to meet your potential results in disappointment and acceptance of mediocrity. Mediocrity and a purposeful life are at odds with each other. Therefore, a purposeful and meaningful life must include a desire to learn and grow each day.

The best description of hell I ever heard was this: "We will experience hell when we someday meet the person we could have become."

Gordon B. Hinckley, former president of The Church of Jesus Christ of Latter-day Saints and a lifelong learner himself, wrote, "There are few things more pathetic than those who have lost their curiosity and sense of adventure, and who no longer care to learn."[3]

WE LEARN WHEN WE OBSERVE OTHERS

Learning happens through many media and forms. Perhaps the most powerful and impactful form of learning is observing others. That is how we do most of our learning as children. In fact, we probably learn at a faster clip between birth and the age of six than we do at any other time in our lives. We learn to speak a language. We learn how to interact with others. We begin to role-play according to how we see the world around us.

Probably the most impactful thing in our learning development is how we observe our parents interacting and living their lives. We oftentimes develop their mannerisms and even adopt speech patterns similar to theirs. While some of that may be genetic, we also tend to adopt their worldview by embracing their political, philosophical, and even religious views.

The older I become, the more I laugh about how much my wife and I and our friends resemble our parents—both in how we look and in how we talk and behave. For my wife's birthday a few years ago, one of her friends sent a card with a picture of some forty-something women, circa 1955, standing on the beach in bathing suits. Most were slightly overweight and had plenty of wrinkles and sagging body parts that commonly afflict middle-aged women. When she opened up the card, it proclaimed, "It's official. We have become our mothers!"

When I was working in athletics, I was fascinated to interact with several volleyball coaches who had played for and learned under the legendary Coach Carl McGown. Carl had won a national championship at BYU and had helped coach the US National Men's Volleyball team for many years. The thing I noticed right away was that most of these coaches who had played for Carl had picked up his mannerisms. They talked like he did with certain intonations and accents on words, behaved like he did on the sidelines, and had become Carl in many ways. I always considered that a compliment to Carl that he had had such an impact on them that they subconsciously adopted his manner of being.

The other day, I was speaking with a teacher who asked me what had been the thing that had best prepared me for the responsible work positions I have held. I thought about his question for a moment and then responded: "I would say it was my various bosses. I have had some amazing mentors at work over the years who taught me by their examples. I observed the good things they did and, occasionally, the things they did that I didn't particularly care for. Some had great people skills. Others were excellent managers. Others were great leaders. I tried to adopt what I considered to be the best of each of them to develop my leadership style."

Throughout my life, I have tried to identify people I consider to be exceptional and amazing and whose lifestyle I want to emulate. I previously mentioned my personal Hall of Fame that included people who have taught me by the way they chose to live their lives. I have watched those people and others closely to see how they interact with others and live their lives. I then try to duplicate the desirable behaviors I observe to the extent that I can. We never become too old to learn from watching and interacting with others.

READING OPENS THE DOORWAY TO LEARNING

When we talk about lifelong learning, probably the first thing that comes to mind is reading. Reading and learning are practically synonyms. To me, it is sad to see how reading has taken a back seat to television in our society. In a previous chapter, I pointed out the amount of time Americans are wasting in front of the TV and computer screens. Yes, you can learn while watching TV or surfing the web, but it is a passive form of learning—not the same as you experience while reading. TV has become the de facto learning method for a huge percentage of Americans, although recent trends happily indicate a fairly significant increase in reading among young people.

When society quits reading books, one of the fallouts is a deterioration of communication skills. I frequently interact with business leaders who bemoan that many—perhaps most—college graduates today don't know how to speak or write well. They can't spell or string together coherent sentences to make a paragraph. Spelling isn't such a big deal nowadays because of spell-checker tools, but the lack of grammatical understanding and the ability to formulate sentences is a major hurdle to good writing.

A local chamber of commerce in Utah recently conducted a survey of many key employers in our state to find out the skills most needed for the current workforce. What they found was that the skills most desired and needed in the workforce are the "soft" skills of communicating well and solving problems. The other skills are important, but employers are looking for employees who can think well, work in teams, solve problems, and communicate effectively.[4]

Over the years, I have taught many communication classes at the university level. I stress to the students the importance of learning to write and communicate well. I tell the students that the world will always have need of exceptional writers and speakers. Unlike some skills that require innate artistic ability, writing well can be learned. I always teach my students that if they want to be good writers, they need to do two things: read a lot and write a lot.

The famous horror author Stephen King understands this well. He has said: "If you don't have time to read, you don't have the time (or the tools) to write. Simple as that."[5]

And speaking of writing, I am a believer that the more we write, the better we become at it. One of the best exercises for regular writing is keeping a journal. Ideally, we take a little time each day to write about our thoughts and dealings. Not only will it give us and our posterity a great look back at what happened in our lives, but also it will provide us with a regular opportunity to practice writing.

My high school classmate, Kevin Hall, recently wrote a book entitled *Aspire*. In it, he explains that in old French, *journèe* meant "a day's travel." *Journal* means "a day." When we write in our journals, we are recording our travels throughout the day.

There have been times in my life when I wrote daily in my journal. As my daily schedule has become more hectic, however, I have chosen to write weekly. Every Sunday, I take about half an hour to comb through the events of the last week. I write my feelings and thoughts in addition to the activities and meetings I have participated in. Thanks to the ease of online journal writing, I also am able to include photos to accompany the copy.

A few years ago, I compiled the life history of my grandmother. She was born in a small town in southern Utah near the turn of the twentieth century. On the surface, her life may have seemed fairly nondescript. However, she was a prolific journal writer and a great example of a lifelong learner. I loved reading about her thoughts and activities and her simple, yet profound, life in the desert of southern Utah and Nevada.

By the time I finished compiling all her journals, they produced a three hundred–page book containing an abundance of stories, both funny and tragic. I got to know her and appreciate the trials and hardships and the joys and successes of her life. Because she had written in her journal and I had published it, she and her memory had not perished from future generations. She had lived a purposeful life that would continue to inspire and teach her offspring for generations to come because she had made the effort to keep a journal.

Benjamin Franklin once wrote, "If you would not be forgotten as soon as you are dead and rotten, either write something worth reading or do things worth the writing."[6]

One of my favorite authors is Ray Bradbury. I once heard him give a speech and was impressed at the effort he undertook to become a great writer. He said he participated in a daily writing exercise to stretch his mind and help develop his writing skills.

Robert Louis Stevenson made this comment: "All through my boyhood and youth . . . I kept always two books in my pocket, one to read and one to write in."[7]

The repeated act of writing teaches us to distill our thoughts and think more clearly. Whenever I have needed to fully grasp a difficult concept, I have tried to put it in writing. Writing has a way of requiring us to focus our mind and think more deeply.

Francis Bacon understood the role writing plays in helping to focus and prepare the mind for crisp thinking. He explained it this way: "Reading maketh a full man; conference a ready man; and writing an exact man."[8]

TECHNOLOGY HAS MADE WRITING EASY

Given today's computers, writing has never been easier. I am writing this chapter while flying on an airplane. Our forefathers needed pen and paper to write. Our parents had access to a typewriter to put their thoughts down on paper. We have computers, tablets, and handheld devices at our disposal. We even have apps that will record our voice and transcribe what we say into written words. There really is no good excuse not to write.

One concern I have, however, is that much of what we write today is easily lost in cyberspace. We send emails today instead of writing letters on paper. We text our thoughts rather than write them on cards. Once we or the recipient hit the delete button, those words and thoughts are gone forever.

Much of our nation's early history was pieced together by historians who accessed letters written by the Founding Fathers to each other and to their family members. John Adams and Thomas Jefferson were prolific letter writers and noted in those letters many of the details of our nation's birth. Imagine Pulitzer Prize-winning author David McCullough trying to write the biography of John Adams without having access to his letters to Abigail, his wife, or to other prominent figures. I am currently reading another McCullough classic biography about Harry Truman. Much of what is known about Truman's early life in Missouri comes from letters he wrote.

Before the advent of email and unlimited cell phone calling, I served an internship in New York City. My first son, Chris, had been born three weeks before I left for the Big Apple. During the two months I spent in New York, my wife and I communicated primarily by letter, supplemented by a weekly phone call. My wife, thankfully, kept the letters she received from me. Many years later, she was looking through some things and came upon the box containing those letters. Reading them brought back a flood of memories to both of us, because in them I described what I was experiencing in New York City and expressed how much I missed the company of her and my infant son.

As we thumbed through the letters, we found one I had written to Chris. Though he was only a couple of months old, I had written him a letter sharing with him my deepest hopes and aspirations for his life and well-being. I was a homesick father who wanted to hold his infant son and had envisioned for him all the wonderful things fathers wish for their sons.

To be truthful, I had completely forgotten about the letter when Nancy found it in the box. Coincidentally, when we discovered the letter, Chris had recently become a new father himself, and his son was about the same age Chris had been when I originally penned the letter from New York. I was certain that when I gave the letter to Chris, it would have double impact. He would be able to understand my emotions about being a new father—something he was currently experiencing—and would be able to empathize with my hopes and aspirations for him when he was a little baby.

An occasional look back at our journals can give us great perspective in our lives. We can see how we overcame trials and obstacles, and we can measure how far we have come. I have often been surprised at how easily emotions and memories return as I read about my past.

Shortly after my daughter was married, she and her husband came to our house one evening. They were both upset. Apparently, my son-in-law had been led to believe he would be getting a promotion at work. When the time came for the company to make the changes, however, he did not get the job nor the salary increase that would come with it. Both he and my daughter were distraught and were wondering how they could go forward now that this opportunity had vanished.

As I listened to their concerns, I remembered how my wife and I had gone through something similar years before when we were first married.

My wife had been a finalist for a teaching job and was preparing to quit her other employment so she could go to work as a teacher. At the last minute, however, she was informed she did not get the teaching job.

At the time, we thought our world had imploded. We didn't know what we were going to do or how we were going to survive financially, especially since we were expecting our first child and planning on the maternity insurance that would come with the teaching job. To us, the future looked dark and bleak at that point.

After listening to our daughter and her husband share their concerns, I went into our den and pulled out my journal. I thumbed through the pages and, sure enough, I found where I had written about that trial in our lives many years ago and the feelings we were going through at that difficult time. I read those words to my daughter and her husband so they could understand that we could relate to what they were experiencing but also to help them see that, while the immediate situation looked depressing, things would get better and they would be okay.

A little later that evening, my daughter came into our room and thanked me for sharing those thoughts. It was comforting to her and her husband to know that we had faced a similar trial when we were their age and had come through it no worse for the wear. The fact that I had read from my journal the exact feelings they were experiencing at the time made it even more impactful than if I had merely recounted the experience.

After my daughter left, my wife turned to me and said, "You know, I had completely forgotten about that experience all those years ago. How did you remember it?"

I don't know what caused me to remember that event in our lives, but I was grateful I had taken the time to write my thoughts in my journal some twenty-five years previously.

One of my great bosses was Glen Tuckett. He served as BYU's athletic director for over a decade and a half. At his retirement press conference, he joked, "Many people ask me what I'm going to do now that I'm retired. I tell them I am planning to finish my book. They say, 'Glen, we didn't know you are writing a book.' To which I respond, 'I'm not. I'm reading one!'"

Reading opens our imaginations and our minds to new ideas and thoughts. Yes, reading takes time, especially when you read as slowly as I do. It is active learning, as opposed to the passive learning we experience with TV. But the rewards stemming from reading are tremendous. I love the story of the young girl who told her teacher she enjoyed reading books more than watching TV. When her teacher asked why, the girl responded, "Because the pictures are better in the books." In other words, the images conjured up by the girl's imagination while reading the book were more vivid and real than the images shown on TV.

I am reluctant to watch a movie that is based on a novel I have already read. One reason is that I have in my mind's eye what the characters and the book's setting look like. When I see the movie, I have to forfeit those perceptions to the director's choice of actors and scenery. A good example is Harry Potter. When you first read *Harry Potter*, you probably had an image of what the young man looked like in your mind. After having seen the movie, however, you probably now picture Harry as Daniel Radcliffe, the young man who plays him in the movies.

READING PARENTS ARE MORE VALUABLE THAN CASKETS OF JEWELS

There is plenty of empirical evidence showing the single most important thing parents can do to help their child acquire language skills, prepare their child for school, and instill a love of learning in their child is to read to them. Reading to a child is one of the easiest ways to prevent future learning problems, and yet many people do not fully understand the enormous, positive impact that this simple act has on the life of a child. Across the United States, just under half (47.8 percent) of all children five and under are read to every day, which means that over thirteen million children go to bed at night without a bedtime story.

One of the most classic poems of all time, written by Strickland Gillilan, is called "The Reading Mother." Its message conveys the value of a mother or parent who takes time to read to children.

The Reading Mother
By Strickland Gillilan

I had a mother who read to me
Sagas of pirates who scoured the sea,
Cutlasses clenched in their yellow teeth,
"Blackbirds" stowed in the hold beneath.

I had a mother who read me lays
Of ancient and gallant and golden days;
Stories of Marmion and Ivanhoe,
Which every boy has a right to know.

I had a mother who read me tales
Of Gelert the hound of the hills of Wales,
True to his trust till his tragic death,
Faithfulness blent with his final breath.

I had a mother who read me the things
That wholesome life to the boy heart brings—
Stories that stir with an upward touch,
Oh, that each mother of boys were such!

You may have tangible wealth untold;
Caskets of jewels and coffers of gold.
Richer than I you can never be—
I had a mother who read to me.[9]

READERS ARE LEADERS

A close friend of mine, Rogan Taylor, who happened to be a best man at my wedding, posted on his Facebook page on December 31 the list of books he had read in 2014. There were thirty-three books on the list, including some like *Les Misérables* that would have been long reads. I was both jealous and inspired as I looked at what he had put into his mind during a year's time.

Dr. Seuss, the children's author, would have been proud of Rogan. In his book, *I Can Read with my Eyes Shut*, he says, "The more that you read, the more things you will know. The more that you learn, the more places you'll go."[10]

In Kevin Hall's book, *Aspire*, he mentions a study done by the Franklin-Covey company to determine why certain people in the company were top producers, making hundreds of thousands of dollars and others were making a mere fraction of that amount. After all the interviews and research, the consultants came back with a three-word analysis: earners are learners.[11]

Those top performers were avid learners who were constantly absorbing new information. They read on average over two dozen books a year.

They knew their customers and understood their needs. They were experts on the products they were selling. They continually tried to upgrade their knowledge and understanding of all things.

Kevin also makes the interesting and accurate assessment that "readers are leaders, and leaders are readers."[12]

One of the things I feel badly about is the decline of newspapers around the world. I understand that we can still access the news on our computers, phones, and tablets, but the fact is that most people don't do that. It used to be that people would start the day at breakfast eating cereal and reading the newspaper. They could scan it and read the stories that interested them before they went off to work.

I recently attended a meeting at which the legendary news reporter Dan Rather spoke. He mentioned how important newspapers were in his intellectual development. His father, he said, referred to newspapers as "a poor man's university."[13]

I read recently about a survey[14] that shows the younger generations are getting their news almost exclusively from social media. In one sense, that is okay. In another sense, it is not good. The news filtered through social media is often incomplete and tends to be filtered to the point of view of the recipient. Another drawback is that rarely does social media deal in depth with issues like local politics. That may explain why there is such illiteracy among the younger population regarding current civic and political events.

The good news is we have more options now than ever before to get news. We have radio, TV, newspapers, magazines, and the Internet. People have the ability to access news on their desktop computers, their laptops, their tablets, or their handheld devices. News has never been more readily available. Now we need to find a way to plug more people into the news so they will become engaged in society.

SET A GOAL TO LEARN SOMETHING EVERY DAY

Some people have a natural curiosity to learn. They are always asking questions and absorbing information. For others, learning is more laborious. They have to work at it. Real learning requires effort and energy. Sometimes it requires sacrifice.

My wife once attended a teacher's seminar. One of the presenters, Marsha Tate, told those in attendance she set a goal every year to learn something substantive. For instance, one year she had learned a foreign language. Another year she had learned calculus. She was determined to be a lifelong learner and continually improve her mind. She was in her sixties at the time and was still going strong in her pursuit of wisdom and learning.

Another friend of mine, Paul James, was the radio "voice" of the BYU Cougars for many years. Late in his life, he learned to play the piano at a very high level. Then he went on to become an accomplished water-paint artist. He was also one of

My wife and I made this rocking horse out of cherry, maple, and walnut while taking a woodworking class.

the most well-read people I knew. He would share with me the titles of the best books he read.

It is never too late in life to learn new skills. A few years ago, my wife and I decided to take a woodworking class together. We signed up for the class and finished some fun projects together. People would express surprise when we told them we were taking a woodworking class. I didn't find it that unusual, but I suppose some people assumed we were too old to take up a new hobby like woodworking. I have enjoyed it so much, I plan to build a woodshop at my house so I can devote more time to it.

USE IT OR LOSE IT

I am a firm believer in the "use it or lose it" theory regarding our memory and mental capacity. If we challenge and stretch our minds, we can do remarkable things and harness their amazing capacity.

When I left to serve an LDS mission in Santiago, Chile, I first spent two months at the Language Training Mission (now called Missionary Training Center) learning Spanish and memorizing the missionary lessons in Spanish. It was a structured environment, and we were constantly learning and memorizing. From sunup to sundown, we were filling our minds with (literally) foreign material.

I set a goal of memorizing all eight of the missionary discussions in Spanish. These amounted to dozens of pages of dialogue. It would have been a lofty goal to memorize them in English, but I was determined to do it in Spanish. In addition, I wanted to memorize a number of scriptures in Spanish so I could use them when needed.

I soon discovered how mentally taxing it was to spend several hours a day memorizing material. But I also learned that the more I did it and focused my mind, the easier it became. I was learning how to tap my mind's almost-limitless potential. By the time I left the LTM two months later, I had accomplished my goal of having memorized all eight discussions. I also realized that I had developed an almost-photographic memory. I could read something and repeat it almost word for word. My mind could capture information and recall it practically at will.

At the end of those two months, I felt more alert and alive than I have ever felt in my life. I guess it was somewhat like actor John Travolta felt in the movie *Phenomenon* when a growing brain tumor somehow opened the potential of his mind and allowed him to learn at prodigious rates and think more clearly than he had ever previously experienced. I felt as if I could learn anything and grasp any concept. My mind was functioning at an extremely high level (for me).

After I left the LTM and arrived in Chile, it didn't take me long to realize how quickly I began to lose the mental edge I had acquired over the previous couple of months. I still spent time each day memorizing and learning, but it was on a much smaller scale. I could tell a difference in my mind's capacity. It was then I came to the realization that our mind is like every muscle in our body. The more we work it, the stronger and healthier it becomes. When we don't use it, it atrophies and shrinks in its ability to do its job.

Whenever one of his players would give an excuse for doing something wrong, one of my coaches would always reply, "Excuses are like bellybuttons: everybody has one."

We all have excuses about why we don't dedicate ourselves to learning more and developing our talents, but those excuses don't fly. The return on investment for time spent reading, writing, learning to play the piano, learning to dance, or participating in other intellectually challenging and stimulating activities will be significant. Determine today to learn something new. Then go do it. You will be better equipped to make a difference in the world and gain increased happiness.

NOTES

1. Albert Einstein, as quoted on Goodreads, accessed September 29, 2015, https://www.goodreads.com/quotes/23863-intellectual-growth-should-commence-at-birth-and-cease-only-at.

2. Genelle Pugmire, "Provo Couple Celebrate 70 Years Together," *Provo Daily Herald*, December 15, 2012.

3. Gordon B. Hinckley, *Way to Be!: 9 Rules for Living the Good Life*, (Simon & Schuster, 2009).

4. Sandy Chamber of Commerce Education Workforce Alliance, "Bridging the Gap," accessed September 29, 2015, http://sandychamber.com/education-workforce-alliance/.

5. NPR Books, "Stephen King: The 'Craft' of Writing Horror Stories," July 2, 2010, http://www.npr.org/templates/story/story.php?storyId=128239303.

6. The Franklin Institute, "Benjamin Franklin FAQ," accessed September 29, 2015, http://learn.fi.edu/franklin/.

7. Robert Louis Stevenson, *Memories and Portraits* (West Roxbury, MA: B&R Samizdat Express, 2015).

8. Francis Bacon, "Of Studies," 1625, accessed September 29, 2015, http://grammar.about.com/od/60essays/a/studiesessay.htm.

9. Strickland Gillilan, "The Reading Mother," accessed September 29, 2015, http://www.yourdailypoem.com/listpoem.jsp?poem_id=352.

10. Dr. Seuss, *I Can Read With My Eyes Shut* (New York City: Random House, 1978).

11. Kevin Hall, *Aspire: Discovering Your Purpose Through the Power of Words* (West Jordan, UT: Bookwise Publishing, 2009), 116.

12. Ibid., 119.

13. Dan Rather, "Dan's Story," accessed September 29, 2015, http://www.danrather.com/story/.

14. Martha Irvine, "Survey: Young adults do consume news, in their own way," Associated Press, March 16, 2015.

seek spiritual balance

WE ARE NOT HUMAN BEINGS HAVING A SPIRITUAL EXPERIENCE. WE ARE SPIRITUAL BEINGS HAVING A HUMAN EXPERIENCE.[1]

—PIERRE TEILHARD DE CHARDIN

From the beginning of time, mankind has sought to commune with and better understand a creator or higher power. Almost every culture has at its root a belief in some sort of supreme being or deity.

Today there are hundreds of organized religions in the world to help people satisfy their innate desire to draw closer to their maker; however, it bears noting that religiosity does not necessarily translate into spirituality.

Religions are built around fundamental doctrines and cultures. They are designed to help people worship in an organized manner, to administer sacred rituals and sacraments and to interact with their fellow men. Spirituality, on the other hand, is very much an individual thing. It can be defined as a person's feelings and sensitivities toward a higher power and holy things. It is possible for a person to be religious but not spiritual, and vice versa. The level of devotion people have toward God varies greatly, even in the same religion. I heard a church talk recently where someone described it this way: Some people *believe* in God. Some people *worship* God. Some people *serve* God.

There have always been and always will be plenty of people who loudly proclaim that religion is a sham—a farce—and that they can be happier living unfettered by religious restrictions. Some go so far as to label religion and spirituality a mental illness. They love to preach their gospel of unbelief. In reality, atheism is its own version of religion—one void of belief in God, but a religion nonetheless.

I, along with countless others—including many researchers—believe just the opposite of the nonbelievers. My personal experience and my experience observing others has convinced me that, generally, people with a spiritual anchor in their lives tend to be happier, better adjusted, and more dedicated to serving others around them. In other words, people in tune with their spiritual selves are able to live more purposeful and joyful lives.

Faith, which typically is a byproduct of spirituality and religion, helps people look to the future and pursue their noblest desires. A key to living a purposeful life is the ability to look ahead and set a course to create a desired outcome. That is more easily done with a compass of faith.

For those who are reluctant to accept my "unscientific" analysis of the role of spirituality and religious involvement in a meaningful and purposeful life, a recent systematic review of 850 research papers on the topic found that "the majority of well-conducted studies found that higher levels of religious involvement are positively associated with indicators of psychological well-being (life satisfaction, happiness, positive affect, and higher morale) and with less depression, suicidal thoughts and behavior, drug/alcohol use/abuse."[2]

The Mayo Clinic, on its website, has an article entitled, "Spirituality and stress relief: Make the connection." The article points out that "spirituality has many benefits for stress relief and overall mental health." Among the ways spirituality can help relieve stress, the article points out, includes feeling a sense of purpose, connecting to the world, releasing control, expanding your network, and leading a healthier life.[3]

Common sense would indicate that teenagers who have a faith in God and participate in religious worship would have less serious legal and societal problems than those who don't. And research backs that up. A recent study found that students who reported high levels of religious participation—attending services one time per week or more—were half as likely to have contemplated suicide.[4]

Another 2014 study of 320 children, ages 8 to 12, in both public and private schools found that, "the more spiritual the child was, the happier the child was."[5]

Religion and spirituality can serve as an anchor for people of all ages in what are tumultuous and troubling times. It is true that religion may not have all the answers to all the questions and problems in our lives. It is also a fact that religious extremism can be a source of many problems in our world. But for many people, religion provides the hope to continue moving forward in times of adversity.

Religion has always played a key role in my life—especially as a young boy growing up in the 1960s and '70s. Our family was churchgoing and very religious. My father and mother insisted that we pray twice a day as a family and that we say personal prayers morning and night. There were no worthy excuses.

It is always fun for the Hale siblings to gather around and share stories about growing up and being "encouraged" to pray. My sister likes to tell the story about the time the family was running late in the morning, and she was in danger of being late for school. Unfazed by my sister's pleadings to let her go, our father called everyone together to pray.

Sure enough, she was late for school and arrived in an empty hallway with the principal standing there to greet her. The principal, who was a member of our church congregation and a friend of my father, asked her to go to his office, where he asked why she was late. I chuckle when I envision my sister sitting in the principal's office explaining that she was late because our father made her stay and pray with the family.

AMERICANS ARE LESS RELIGIOUS BUT PRAY MORE

Recent studies have shown that Americans are slowly turning away from organized religion. The Pew Research Center did a study[6] that showed the number of religiously unaffiliated in America between 2007 and 2014 grew by 6 percent. That means approximately fifty-six million adults claim no religion. But while we are not as interested in organized religion, Americans continue to be a prayerful people. A 2014 study[7] shows that 57 percent of us pray at least once a day. That is actually up slightly from 1983, when only 53 percent prayed daily. And 75 percent of people claim to pray at least once a week, while 25 percent say they pray less often or never.

I acknowledge that a person can be happy and live a fulfilling, meaningful life without believing in God or a higher power. However, I believe that living with purpose is more easily achieved when accompanied by faith, hope, and acceptance that a higher power is in charge and holds us accountable for our actions. I agree with the observation previously cited that "happy is the [person] who has found . . . [his or her] worship and loves [it]."

Studies show that 71 percent of Americans believe in God or a universal spirit. We are, after all, a nation "under God." Unfortunately, as noted above, the number of churchgoers continues to decline as religion comes under attack from government, academia, Hollywood, courts, and the media. It is becoming increasingly difficult to pick up a newspaper without reading about some sort of attack on believers. The result is that we have an increasingly Godless country and people with less spiritual guidance and balance in their lives. Many people, including me, believe the drop in America's practice of religion coincides directly with the decline in our societal norms and values and an increase in many of society's woes.

The good news is that many institutions, including universities, are rediscovering the critical need for education that focuses on developing the whole person: body, mind, *and* spirit.

Religion played a critical role in the establishment of many universities and educational institutions throughout the world. However, for the past five or six decades, religion and all things spiritual have been pushed out of academia. It was assumed spirituality and critical thinking were incompatible. In fact, those who believe in and practice their religion have often been ridiculed by professors and classmates.

Gradually, some universities have acknowledged that education of the whole being requires a spiritual component. Students who noticed that spirituality has been AWOL on campuses have begun to request classes dealing with spiritual topics. The result has been that some universities have become more inclusive of religiosity and spirituality. A few have gone so far as to create reflection centers where students can pray and enjoy peaceful meditation.

8——

The two years I spent in Chile as a missionary were supremely transformative years for me. I went to Chile as a teenager struggling to know what to do with my life. For two years I taught people about God and faith. There were those we met who were people of faith and were content with their lifestyle and religion. Others were agnostic and had given up on God and religion. Still others were confused and searching for meaning and purpose in their lives. We spent most of our time working with the last group.

It was fascinating to witness the change in the lives of people from all walks of life when they began to experience a portion of faith and hope, when the spiritual stirrings inside them began to awake. Time after time I saw people who were discouraged and depressed about their lives become animated and excited about living and moving forward after they found faith. I saw despair replaced by hope. I saw anger and animosity replaced with love and peace.

I met people whose lives were transformed in dramatic fashion. One man, who had a great job as the photo-finish cameraman at the horse racetrack quit his job because he felt the environment was not conducive to his new beliefs and lifestyle. It was a tremendous leap of faith for him and his family to walk away from that job, but he was happy to do it. Having spirituality in his life was more important to that man than having material things. I recently received a Facebook message from one of his sons telling me that both he and his son (the grandson of the father I taught) had served as missionaries. The grandson is now in the United States preparing to enter a university. Three generations of the same family have been dramatically impacted by the father's decision to add faith to his life.

Some people experience spirituality through means other than religion. A trip into nature is a spiritual experience of sorts for many, including me. I cannot climb a mountain or view the grandeur of nature without being buoyed in spirit. When my wife and I are in the wilderness, we commune with nature and feel closer to our Creator.

Thomas Blount said, "Every flower of the field, every fiber of a plant, every particle of an insect, carries with it the impress of its Maker, and can—if duly considered—read us lectures of ethics or divinity."[8]

Dante put it this way: "Nature is art of God eternal."[9]

I grew up near a Navajo Indian reservation. I have always admired the Navajo people and their respect for nature. They try to be at peace and harmony with the world (Mother Earth) around them at all times. This is called "walking in beauty." Their spirituality draws its strength from the earth.

One of the benefits that comes from religion and spirituality is hope. There is a peace and assurance that comes from faith in a higher being and belief that life has a purpose greater than our own life. Many times I have had to rely on hope to get through difficult situations like deaths of loved ones and professional setbacks. Knowing that I could trust in God to help me through those experiences was a great comfort to me.

As I write this chapter, a community near me is struggling with teenage suicide. Two young people committed suicide during the week, and a third unsuccessfully attempted it. Parents and teachers are deeply concerned and want answers. Teen suicide is a huge problem in our society.

A friend of mine, Greg Hudnall, is head of a group called Hope4Utah that attempts to educate communities about ways to identify signs of suicidal tendencies. His program has made a huge difference in decreasing teen suicides wherever it has been implemented. The program has a list of things that help with suicide prevention—things like positive relationships with family, friends, school, or other caring adults. One of the key connections is religious and spiritual beliefs about the meaning and value of life.

SPIRITUAL PEOPLE LOOK DIFFERENT

Throughout my life, I have noticed a very real difference in the countenances of those who have deep spirituality in their lives and those who don't. Sometimes it is manifest through a smile, but more often it is light in the eyes.

On one occasion, I was attending a college basketball tournament and was watching a game between two teams from another state. During timeouts, the cheerleaders would go out and dance on the floor. I noticed that one cheerleader in particular had a different look than the others. Her smile and countenance were brighter. She radiated inner confidence and beauty. It was very noticeable.

I turned to a member of the media sitting next to me and asked him if one of the cheerleaders looked different to him. He correctly identified the same young woman I had noticed. After the game, I approached the young lady and started a conversation. She told me she was a deeply religious person with strong spiritual beliefs. Her answer confirmed to me that her spirituality actually displayed itself in her countenance.

On another occasion, I was in a post office in Santiago, Chile. There were dozens of people waiting in line with me. A woman walked in the door and stood among the throng of bodies. As soon as I saw her, it was as if her countenance lit up the room. She was noticeably different than everyone else in the room, although she was doing nothing to draw attention to herself. I was so impressed by the stark contrast of her look compared to the others that I waited for her to go through the line. I introduced myself and started a conversation with her. She conveyed to me that she was a devoutly religious person, which confirmed my suspicion and reinforced my theory that people with strong religious backgrounds have a different look than others.

SPIRITUALITY HELPS US DEAL WITH LIFE'S ADVERSITY

Life brings many challenges and moments of adversity our way. We have trials in our familial relationships. We have trials at work. Sometimes we have health challenges. We experience incredible trials from losing loved ones.

My experience has shown me that a strong spiritual foundation can help us weather those challenges and will also give us confidence as we interact with others during our journey through life.

As previously mentioned, living purposefully means we live with a goal and plan in mind that will, hopefully, lead to a more joyful and meaningful life. Such a purposeful lifestyle can be achieved without spirituality, but it is much harder, and it will not be at the same level as the life that is wrapped in genuine spirituality.

NOTES

1. Pierre Teilhard De Chardin and Ursula King, *Pierre Teilhard De Chardin: Writings* (Maryknoll, NY: Orbis Books, 1999).

2. Alexander Moreira-Almeida, Francisco Lotufo Neto, and Harold G. Koenig, "Religiousness and mental health: a review," Rev. Bras. Psiquiatr. 28, no. 3 (2006): 242–50.

3. Mayo Clinic Staff, "Spirituality and stress relief: Make the connection," accessed September 29, 2015, http://www.mayoclinic.org/healthy-lifestyle/stress-management/in-depth/stress-relief/art-20044464.

4. *Provo Daily Herald*, "New data show family, religious activity protect youth from suicide ideation," March 12, 2015, http://www.heraldextra.com/sanpete-county/new-data-show-family-religious-activity-protect-youth-from-suicide/article_bfeabc09-9aa0-5846-964e-492fd8e5dc80.html.

5. Mark D Holder, Ben Coleman, Judi M. Wallace, "Spirituality, Religiousness, and Happiness in Children Aged 8–12 Years," *Journal of Happiness Studies* 11, no. 2 (2010): 131–150.

6. "America's Changing Religious Landscape," Pew Research Center, May 12, 2015, http://www.pewforum.org/2015/05/12/americas-changing-religious-landscape/.

7. Scott Clement, "Americans continue to pray even as religious practices wither, survey says," *Washington Post*, March 6, 2015.

8. Stephen Harrod Buhner, *The Secret Teachings of Plants: The Intelligence of the Heart in the Direct Perception of Nature* (Rochester, NY: Bear & Company, 2004), 263.

9. Dante, quoted in "Inspirational Nature Quotes," accessed September 29, 2015, http://www.spiritual-quotes-to-live-by.com/nature-quotes.html.

conclusion

You now are familiar with the seven keys for purposeful living. As I mentioned in the introduction, these keys are not earth shattering or even particularly novel. They are merely time-tested true principles that, if followed, will lead to a life that is more meaningful, fulfilling, impactful, and joyful.

Living a purposeful life is a choice. It is an attitude. It requires some degree of sacrifice. It requires focus and direction and passion. Purposeful living is just that—purposeful. It includes the workplace but extends beyond it. It includes the home but extends beyond that as well. A truly purposeful life cannot be segmented into parts. Our life's purpose is the sum total of who and what we are and the impact we have on the world in which we live.

Here are some final thoughts and questions for you to consider about each of the keys. As you ask yourself the questions, be honest in your answers. Know that the keys themselves will not make your life more purposeful—only putting them into action will create an opportunity for you to live a life that matters more both to yourself and to others.

KEY #1: BE A DOER, NOT A SPECTATOR

- Making a difference requires action and energy—the antithesis of spectating.
- Decide now to limit those things in your life that don't produce a return on investment for the time you spend on them. Television and excessive time in front of a computer screen would be good places to start as you do an inventory of wasted time.
- Resolve to do both spontaneous and planned activities with your friends and loved ones in order to create lasting memories. Do not

procrastinate. The clock is ticking on your life and the lives of your family members.

- Don't wait for tomorrow or some future event to be happy. Take advantage of today. Relish and make the most of each moment you are given.

Questions to Ask Yourself

1. What can I do in my life that will help me make better use of my time?
2. How can I use that extra time to make a difference in my community or in my family?
3. What activities can I plan with my family and friends to create memories and opportunities for service?

KEY #2: CULTIVATE MEANINGFUL RELATIONSHIPS

- Nothing is more important or valuable in life than our relationships.
- Most of the good effectuated in the world is done at the interpersonal level. That is where the average person can have the biggest impact.
- Familial relationships are critical to our happiness and development. How children are treated by parents plays a critical role in how children develop as adults.
- How we relate to and interact with friends and coworkers will establish our personal brand and will go a long way toward determining the influence for good we can have in our personal universe.

Questions to Ask Yourself

1. How are my relationships with those I love and care about most?
2. What can I do to be a better spouse, a better son or daughter, or a better sibling?
3. How am I viewed by coworkers and customers or clients? Does my work persona match my private persona?
4. Do I make the effort to be a mentor to those who are looking for help in their lives or professions?
5. What have I done lately to strengthen a valuable relationship?
6. When was the last time I did a kind deed anonymously for someone at work or at home?
7. How do I want to be remembered when I am gone, and what can I do to encourage others to view me in that light?

KEY #3: MAKE A DIFFERENCE IN OTHERS' LIVES

- With a little effort, attention, and sacrifice, we can have a dramatic impact upon the lives of those with whom we associate.
- It is easy to say no, but saying yes is more likely to change lives for the better. Be a person who says yes.
- Having money is not a prerequisite to making a positive impact in our communities; rather, passion and resolve are the key ingredients to being an influence for good.
- When others feel your love and concern, that alone can sometimes motivate them to be a better person and make more of their lives.
- Expect those around you to give their best effort and be their best selves. Don't accept mediocrity. Don't be afraid to challenge yourself.

Questions to Ask Yourself

1. What am I doing to make a positive difference in the lives of those with whom I associate?
2. What sacrifice can I make to help my community be a better place?
3. Whose life would be made better if I were willing to sacrifice a little time, talent, or treasure on their behalf?
4. How have I helped the poor or less fortunate lately?
5. To what charity have I donated time or money in the last six months?
6. Who are three people outside my immediate family whose lives I have positively impacted?

KEY #4: GET ACTIVE AND STAY ACTIVE

- It is hard to make a difference in the world if you don't have the physical ability and energy to put forth the required effort.
- You don't need to run marathons or spend inordinate amounts of time working out in order to keep yourself in good physical condition. The key is regular activity that gets you moving.
- Working out is easier and, often, more enjoyable when done with others.
- Paying money to participate in an athletic competition can serve as a motivator to get in shape.
- If you live an active life before age fifty, it will be easier to maintain an active lifestyle after age fifty.
- Proper diet and regular exercise are keys to reducing obesity.
- The benefits of exercise are more than physical. Improved mental and emotional well-being are byproducts of working out.

Questions to Ask Yourself

1. What can I do in my daily life that will cause me to get more exercise and be more active?
2. When was the last time I committed to participate in a scheduled athletic event of some kind?
3. Who can I ask to join me as a workout partner who will be dependable and motivating?
4. What adjustment can I make to my diet beginning today that will result in positive health benefits?
5. Is there a new activity I would like to learn that would give me another opportunity to get some exercise?

KEY #5: LOVE YOUR WORK

- You are happier and more passionate about making a difference in the workplace when you love your work.
- Sometimes if you want a job you truly love, you may need to accept a lower salary than you could get in another line of work.
- The best way to find purposeful, fulfilling employment is to follow your passion.
- How you leave a job is just as important as how you enter a job.
- If you make the boss look good, you and the entire organization will look good and be more successful.

Questions to Ask Yourself

1. Does my job utilize my best talents and skills?
2. Do I feel like I am making a contribution in my job?
3. How do I utilize my job to make a positive difference in the community?
4. Do I wake up in the morning excited to go to work?
5. Do I take advantage of opportunities to network on a regular basis?
6. Do I spend too much time working? Am I able to unplug when I am home?

KEY #6: BE A LIFELONG LEARNER

- You are never too old to learn new things.
- Highly successful people tend to be avid readers.
- Reading and writing are two things you should do on a regular, if not daily, basis.
- Writing regularly in your journal is a great way to practice writing

skills and keep a record of your life for posterity to enjoy.

- If you don't constantly keep using and exercising your mind, your ability to remember and think will diminish.
- It is never too late to learn something that can make a difference in your community, your family, or at work.
- Those who quit learning essentially quit living.

Questions to Ask Yourself

1. How many good books have I read in the last year?
2. Do I keep a journal? How often do I write in it?
3. When was the last time I learned to do something new (hobby, language, skill, and so on)?
4. What do I do to challenge my mind on a regular basis?
5. When was the last time I memorized something significant?
6. Is there something I have always wanted to learn but have procrastinated learning it for one reason or another?

KEY #7: SEEK SPIRITUAL BALANCE

- Mankind has always had a desire to find spiritual peace.
- Spirituality and religiosity are two different things, although for some people one can lead to the other.
- People with a spiritual anchor in their lives tend to be happier.
- A decline in spirituality and religiosity in the world is contributing to many of the social ills plaguing society today.
- True education must nourish the whole person, including mind, body, and spirit.
- People with spiritual balance in their lives have a happier countenance.

Questions to Ask Yourself

1. What am I doing to find harmony with spiritual things?
2. When was the last time I read something about a spiritual topic?
3. What do I know about universal or fundamental beliefs held by most of the world's religions?
4. Do I take time during the day to commune with nature, meditate, or pray?
5. How much time do I spend each day with nothing competing for my attention (music, radio, coworkers, TV)?
6. What is the foundation of my moral compass in life?

about the author

V al Hale is a doer. Whether serving as athletic director at Brigham Young University; as vice president at Utah Valley University—Utah's largest university; as executive director of the Utah's Governor's Office of Economic Development; as an ecclesiastical leader; or as president of Habitat for Humanity, he has always tried to make a positive difference.

Thanks to the varied experiences he has had and the people he has met through his assignments, Val has observed life from a unique perspective. He has associated with many inspiring people who live purposeful, fulfilling lives. He also has seen those unfortunate souls who are content with mediocrity, or less.

Always a teacher at heart, Val has taken the lessons he has learned in his interactions with people and shares them in this book with the intent to inspire people to become their best selves and find maximum happiness and fulfillment in life.

Born in Snowflake, Arizona, Val experienced his early life in small-town America. Though poor, his large family of nine siblings was full of love. He graduated from Orem High School in Utah and Brigham Young University with bachelor's and master's degrees in public relations and communications. His first job was as a news reporter for the *Provo Daily Herald*. He has been an adjunct faculty member at two universities.

He served as chair of the NCAA Division I Men's Golf Committee, chair and president/CEO of the Utah Valley Chamber of Commerce, president of Riverside Country Club, and he currently sits on more than thirty-five boards of directors, including several nonprofits.

Val and his wife, Nancy, have been married for thirty-six years and have three children and eleven grandchildren.

SCAN TO VISIT

0 26575 17048 1